Essex Pride

by

Stan Jarvis

IAN HENRY PUBLICATIONS

1984

Copyright © Stan Jarvis, 1984

ISBN 0 86025 877 7

Printed in Great Britain
for Ian Henry Publications Ltd
38 Parkstone Avenue, Hornchurch, Essex, RM11 3LW

CONTENTS

EARLY DAYS — 1
The Peasants' Revolt, Roger Ascham, William Hunter, Thomasine Tyler, Thomas Tusser William Gilberd

THE SEVENTEENTH CENTURY — 27
John Bastwick, Samuel Puchas, Mary Honywood, William Kempe, Peter Chamberlen, Henry Winstanley, William Alexander

THE EIGHTEENTH CENTURY — 49
James Oglethorpe, Dick Turpin, Edward Bright, Thomas Plume

THE NINETEENTH CENTURY — 64
Samuel Courtauld, Charles Clark, Frederic Chancellor, Edward Bingham, Richard Sutton Cheek, The Russian Colony, John Salter

THE TWENTIETH CENTURY — 97
Isaac Mead, Frances Maynard, Evelyn Wood, Frank Crittall, Thomas Smith, Jimmy Mason, Laurence Oates, Thomas Clarkson, Dorothy L Sayers, Vic Gunn

DEDICATION

To Hazel,
my dear wife,
with love and thanks

*The Peasants' Revolt − Roger Ascham
− William Hunter − Thomasine Tyler −
Thomas Tusser − William Gilberd*

Great Baddow is not a spot on the tourist's map of England. It is simply a village settled by a tribe so long ago that the name they gave it cannot now be accurately interpreted. If they were the ancient British whom Caesar saw, then the name can be construed as 'the place beside the birch stream', if they were the Saxons who followed the Romans, then the name means 'Battle River', referring to the river now known as the Chelmer, running through the vale sloping gently down from the village.

The Saxons ordered their new country and Baddow became part of the vast estates of Algar, Earl of Mercia, who passed them on to his son, Eadwine. By this time, however, William the Conqueror had made his successful take-over bid and Eadwine tried to organise a rebellion. He was killed and the King, taking over all his lands, vested them in the great monastery and church he was having built at Caen. So, when the Domesday Book was completed in 1086, Baddow was given a full entry, showing that it was then held by that church of the Holy Trinity. We are told the numbers of every class of person and every kind of animal kept by the villagers, right down to 'one horse and one foal'. One part of the entry reads strangely to our eyes: "It then [in the time of King Edward] rendered entertainment for eight nights, now 17 pounds." It means that in Algar the Saxon's time, this village was already saddled with the obligation to raise from its rents and its taxes sufficient money to pay for the lodging and entertainment of the King or his representative for eight nights of the year. The Normans commuted that arrangement to a realistic, but unromantic, seventeen pounds a year.

Let 500 years roll by in the endless cycle of rural life and we find a new owner of Baddow lands, Henry VIII, settling them on Katherine of Aragon as part of her marriage dowry. But in the interim there had been one event that jerked Baddow abruptly out of its peaceful somnulence and into the history books. In 1381 the walls of the church preceding the present building were the backdrop for a scene of noise and confusion. Imagine that sleepy old churchyard teeming with hundreds of people, all talking together in a fever of excitement. This was no grand society wedding, no happy baptism, this was just one manifestation of a full-scale revolt of the people of Essex against the might and majesty of the King and his nobles.

The Peasants' Revolt, as it has come to be known, has taken its place in social history as a significant milestone on the English working man's long road to freedom of labour. Laws had been passed to keep wages down because, since the old system of compulsory labour for the Lord of the Manor had died out, the new smaller farmers, renting land from the Lord, could not afford the wages demanded by the landless labourers. The battle between the factions went on through the years. The terrific death rate caused by the Black Death in 1348-9 caused a labour shortage and gave the peasants bargaining power, and leaders like John Ball and Wat Tyler came forward to express their feelings and there were spontaneous risings in Essex and Kent. D W Coller, writing in 1861, puts the reason:

"A poll-tax of 3 groats a head on all above

the age of 15 gave edge to the uneasy discontent of the degraded and, it may be truly said, the oppressed, populace. This impost had always been one of the most hated of government exactions; and in this instance the attempt to levy it with vigour drove the people to desperation. The ruling powers, pressed by a war with France, for the support of which the poll-tax was professedly laid on, finding it not sufficiently productive, sent out special commissioners to quicken its flow into the Treasury."

In May, 1381, the tax-commissioner Thomas Bampton rode out to Brentwood to hold an inquiry concerning the non-payment of taxes in Essex, particularly by the people of Fobbing, Corringham and Stanford-le-Hope, who, with others, were called to attend. The Fobbing men explained that they had been let off because of their poverty by commissioners who had levied the tax the previous winter. But Bampton was under great pressure to obtain the money. He said their circumstances would be checked again, with a view to the tax being paid. Though he had two soldiers with him, the fishermen of Fobbing were so threatening that Bampton and his men galloped back to London to tell of the revolt.

The big guns were brought up; Sir Robert Belknap, Chief Justice of the King's Bench, was sent out into Essex to restore order, arriving at Brentwood on Whitsunday, 2nd June. He ordered the local jurors to present indictments against the men whose names were known, but a great crowd of protesters threatened the judge and he was forced to swear on the Bible that he would never again undertake such an enquiry. He escaped harm, but three of the poor jurors were beheaded in the fracas and so too were three clerks who served Bampton on that first enquiry. Now the Essex men had totally committed themselves to revolt. They impaled the heads of those unfortunate victims on pikes and carried them before an angry mob that roamed the area gathering support and wreaking vengeance on local tyrants. John Ewell, escheator of the County, who dealt with lands forfeited to the Crown, was beheaded at Langdon Hills; the home of Sir Robert Hales at Cressing was destroyed on 10th June; and the manor house of the Sheriff, John Sewell, at Coggeshall, was broken into and looted. One of the prime aims of the revolutionaries was to destroy all the records, kept at such manor houses, of the local court proceedings, so that precedents for the burdensome duties and fines required of the humble labourers were done away with for ever.

On 11th June, a band of some 30,000 Essex men began their march on London and camped in the fields at Mile End. Wat Tyler put their case to the young King Richard who had come out to meet them at 7 in the morning on Friday, 14th June. The Essex men owned allegiance to the King, but asked for the abolition of serfdom, the freeing of tenants from obligations to their lords, and a general pardon for all those who committed offences in the cause and course of the rebellion. The demands were granted, but, before the new order could be celebrated, Richard called for a further meeting with Tyler and, in full view of his men, Tyler, unarmed, was slain. The disconcerted peasants offered no further resistance, but they were not finished; they confronted the King again at Waltham, where Richard, at the head of his army, went back on his word, "Serfs you have been and are; you shall remain in bondage, not such as you have hitherto been subjected to, but incomparably viler."

So the news was noised around the Essex lanes - the old order remained and the lords would wreak vengeance. The Essex men were well organised. Meetings were called and so it was that Great Baddow churchyard was selected as one of the great rallying points. Men were told that if they did not come and support the rising, their houses would be burnt above their heads. With what trepidation the women of the village must have watched the vast mob of men call for armed resistance to the King and move off to Norsey Wood outside Billericay to take up battle positions along with a great meeting of men from Rettendon. They made an ill-defended camp and waited throughout the night of 27th June behind a barricade of farm carts chained together. Just before dawn the Royal Army attacked and annihilated them. Some 500 homes were fatherless that night. The few surviving rebels made half-hearted attempts to re-form as they retreated, but could not persuade the citizens of Colchester to close their gates against the King and so they fell further back into Suffolk and Huntingdon, where they were finally dispersed.

How many times the tale must have been told at the fireside of inn or alehouse or humble home of that fateful meeting in Baddow churchyard and the fearful consequences! It was the bravery of those unknown, ordinary Essex people that benefited later generations in the struggle for recognition of their right to a decent standard of living.

Walthamstow is no longer part of Essex. In the re-organisation some 25 years ago of local government boundaries, it became part of the new London Borough of Waltham Forest. In the days of the horse, the greatest hazard for the traveller through Walthamstow to and from the great City of London was the River Lea flooding down to Hackney Marshes. Now that river has been canalised and bridged, it is the swirling stream of traffic on the North Circular Road that has to be carefully negotiated. Its proximity to London and the Lea has caused Walthamstow's development as a residential and industrial suburb of London. Even as far back as 1861 David Coller wrote: "Walthamstow adjoins Woodford, on the verge of the forest, and abounds in beautiful woodland scenery, with a tract of marshland towards the Lea, by which river it is separated from Middlesex. Its population, which is that of a good town, and has vastly increased within the last ten years, is scattered over a series of separate villages... There are 13 almshouses and a good free school near the church, in which foundation scholars, for 10s. a quarter, are taught Latin, English, writing and arithmetic..." It is interesting to note that the school was founded by Sir George Monox in 1542, when Roger Ascham, the famous author of **The Scholemaster**, was 27. The connection is that Ascham did actually live in Walthamstow at the time he was working out the plan for this great work.

"Carry no tales, be no common teller of news,

be not inquisitive of other men's talk, for those that are desirous to hear what they need not, commonly be ready to babble what they should not." Such was the sound, commonsense advice given to one of Lord Warwick's servants over four hundred years ago by this man hailed in the **Oxford History of England** as 'the greatest educationist of his time.' Yet Ascham was not a prudish classical scholar – he lived and died a poor man because he was so passionately fond of gambling, on the throw of a dice or on the cockfighting of which he acknowledges his enjoyment in **The Scholemaster.**

Roger Ascham was born in 1515 at Kirby Wiske, near Northallerton, third son of the steward to Lord Scrope of Bolton. He looked up to his father, called him later 'the wisest of men' and was happy to be advised by him to enter, when very young, the household of Sir Anthony Wingfield who, as he described later, 'ever loved and used to have many children brought up in learnynge in his house' along with his own boys. Wingfield recognised Roger's ability and so paid for his further education, from 15 years of age, at St. John's College, Cambridge. Sir Anthony himself taught Roger archery, in which he delighted and later sang its praises in his other famous book, **Toxophilus.** At college he was diligent, much-liked by tutors who became life-long friends, along with fellow students with whom he kept in touch after they became Bishops of Chichester, Winchester and Lincoln, and other luminaries of church and state.

In the course of his education, Ascham became fluent in Greek, familiar with all extant Latin literature, accomplished in music, with more than a nodding acquaintance with mathematics and skilled in penmanship. In July, 1537, he was awarded his M.A. degree and the following year his college appointed him to the Readership in Greek at a good salary and he was able to gather round him a coterie of admiring pupils, some of whom became firm friends. His beautiful calligraphy also brought him employment as official letter-writer to the University.

Just when life seemed set for happiness in comfort and he was on holiday with his proud parents in Yorkshire, Ascham caught a debilitating fever, so bad that he was unable to travel back to his Cambridge college for two whole years. So his money ran out and he came to know the meaning of real poverty. One of his friends, Edward Lee, Archbishop of York, secured him a pension of 40 shillings, whilst he worked on translating important religious works from Greek into Latin.

In 1542 he was able to return to Cambridge, but new troubles crowded in - his brother and his parents died and arguments in the University caused him to have to take sides in bitter disputes. How he wished he could get away from it all, possibly in the service of a gentleman engaged in foreign travel! That was to come later, but at this time he found solace in working on his book on archery. His ambition was to be able to present a copy to his King, Henry VIII, as proof of his patriotism. At first frustrated, the glorious opportunity arrived in 1545 in the gallery at Greenwich. Ascham tells us that Henry was so taken with it that he granted him a pension of ten pounds a year, a wonderful upturn in his fortunes! Of course Henry encouraged the teaching of the martial arts and this book, in vigorous English understandable by the common man, encouraged the practice of archery as an art and an exercise.

The following year Roger Ascham was given the important position of public orator, conducting all its correspondence with outside bodies and writing to important people in his strenuous efforts to win influential support for his University. Almost at the same time he had come to the notice of the Princess Elizabeth as a very able tutor, probably through her then tutor, William Grindal, himself one of Ascham's students and a personal friend. When that friend died, in 1548, Ascham was asked to replace him, and so he had to live at Cheshunt where the princess dwelt for many years under the care of Sir Anthony Denny. He found great joy in Elizabeth's aptitude and in her accomplishment in languages, in writing and in music, for they were all a common interest.

This was a cloistered life, however, and Ascham missed so much the hurly-burly of the University that within two years he was back there, attending to all its correspondence once again. Then he heard of the opportunity to travel abroad as secretary to Sir Richard Morysin, newly appointed ambassador to the Court of Emperor Charles V. He took it and went with the Ambassador to Augsburg, from where it was possible to travel around, including a journey to Venice, before recall in 1553. In a letter to a friend, he said he had had enough of strange countries and customs and just longed to get back to Cambridge and the friendship of his familiar books! No doubt he missed the congeniality of university life, the archery of which he was so fond, and the chance to see a cockfight and back his fancy.

On 1st January, 1554, he married Margaret Howe. He writes of her as a beautiful bride and young for a man 'so well stept into years'. Soon they had a son, Giles, and increasing household expenses. But he had been fortunate to be appointed Latin secretary to Queen Mary, with his pension from the sovereign doubled to £20 and, through the good offices of Sir William Petrie, builder of Ingatestone Hall, he obtained the lease of an estate at Walthamstow, called Salisbury Hall, at a rent equal to that pension.

On Elizabeth's accession Ascham's service was continued and he resumed her royal tutorship. The arrival of two more sons by 1564 brought him further financial difficulties and he had to mortgage Salisbury Hall. But it is a pleasant thought for Essex people that while he was there he found consolation in the planning of his great work on education. The idea may have been brought about by a dinner Ascham had at Windsor with Sir William Cecil, Sir Richard Sackville and others. They had heard the news that certain boys had run away from Eton because they had suffered so much from repeated floggings. Talk at dinner turned on the necessity for discipline in inculcating education. Ascham spoke forcefully against these wicked and unnecessary beatings to such good effect that there and then Sackville said that if Ascham would instruct a teacher in his system he would add him to his household and educate Ascham's boys along with his own. Other friends suggested that he should publish his excellent ideas as a practical guide for schoolmasters.

Ascham at once went to work, drawing up a plan completed in two 'books'. He held that young men should be "... so grounded in judgement of learning, so founded in love of honesty, as, when they should be called forth to the execution of great affairs, in service of their prince and country, they might be able to use and order all experiences... according to the square, rule and line of wisdom, learning and virtue." The first book argued the case, with many instances from his own experience for 'alluring' a child to its education by gentle encouragement, rather than by force. It included his warning of the hazards to be met with by young men in the foreign travel for the completion of education that was then so fashionable. He also pointed out the dangers and moral risk for rich young men living a life of self-indulgence in court circles.

The second book expanded upon the method of teaching Latin in some detail. It would have gone in greater detail into this and other subjects, but illness and death overtook him. On 23rd December, 1568, his sleepless fever developed into a week-long, painful, final illness. He died, aged 54, on 30th December and was buried quietly in St. Sepulchre's Church, London, opposite the Old Bailey. Strangely enough, it was in that same church that another Essex man, William Harvey, propounder of the theory of the circulation of the blood, was married in 1605.

A telling tribute to Ascham's memory is Queen Elizabeth's comment on hearing the news of his death: "I would rather have cast £10,000 into the sea than have lost my Ascham." The great disappointment of the last weeks of his life must have been that he could not see his **Scholemaster** finished and in print. His widow had it published in 1570, exactly as he had left it and it has been constantly reprinted through 400 years.

Though his book can still be read and appreciated, his little Essex estate has gone. It remained intact until 1904, then it was broken up and the Hall, with 141 acres, was sold for development on the continuing expansion of the London suburbs into Walthamstow.

Motorists from Chelmsford, queuing up at the traffic lights at the top of Brentwood's High Street, have more than enough time to look around as the traffic shuffles along and the lights change and change again. Their eyes are caught, on the lefthand side, by the monument on the very edge of the pavement by those lights. It is a brown granite obelisk, looking rather worn, though it has recently been restored. The cracks in the column are not a natural fault in the stone; they were the result of the intense heat when Wilson's, the big furniture shop on the corner, caught fire in 1907. The monument was erected in 1861 and rebuilt in 1910. It commemorates a very much earlier event - and a sad one in our Essex story - the last chapter of an episode that began in 1555 and was judged by John Foxe to be so harrowing as to be worthy of inclusion in the 2nd edition of his work popularly known as **The Book of Martyrs**, published in 1570.

The inscriptions on the four sides of the obelisk sketch the story: "To the pious memory of William Hunter, a native of Brentwood, who, maintaining his right to search the scriptures and in all matters of faith and practice to follow their sole guidance, was condemned at the early age of nineteen, by Bishop Bonner in the reign of Queen Mary, and burned at the stake near this spot, March XXVI, MDLV. He yielded up his life for the truth, sealing it with his blood to the praise of God. Erected by public subscription 1861. This monument was restored after being damaged by fire, September, 1910." "He was tortured, not accepting deliverance, that he might obtain a better resurrection." "William Hunter, Martyr, committed to the flames, March XXVI, MDLV. Christian reader, learn from his example to value the privilege of an open Bible and be careful to maintain it. He being dead yet speaketh." "Be faithful unto death and I will give them the crown of life."

William had been brought up in the Protestant faith by believing, loving parents from his birth in 1534. His faith and his views were already firmly fixed when Mary came to the throne in 1553. She put the failure of her marriage to Philip of Spain down to God's punishment for the heresy of Protestantism still practiced by staunch adherents in England. So her clergy were constrained to be on the watch for heretics and to report them immediately. As soon as she became Queen she ordered that everybody was to go and receive communion at Mass that very Easter. At that time William Hunter was a 19-year-old apprentice weaver in London. He refused to attend as ordered, which put his master in a spot because, as he was responsible for William's behaviour as an apprentice, he would be the target of ecclesiastical wrath. He told Hunter to leave the job until the trouble blew over and William went home to Brentwood to stay with his parents for a couple of months.

One day, as he walked down the High Street, he saw the door to the old chapel was open. He went in and was soon totally absorbed in reading the Bible which he found lying on the priest's desk. It happened that an official of the Bishop of London's court saw him go in, followed him and interrupted his study to ask him just what he thought he was doing. He was surprised that a common apprentice, now unemployed, could read at all and he felt, in any case, that the Bible should be reserved to the minister himself for quotation and interpretation to his congregation. No doubt he knew by report of the young man's obstinate Protestantism, for he said to him, "William, why meddlest thou with the Bible? Understandeth thou what thou readest? Canst thou expound Scripture?" The young man replied humbly enough, "I presume not to expound scripture; but finding the Bible here, I read for my comfort and edification."

The official at once ran off to the priest at South Weald, for in those days that was the parish church for Brentwood. The vicar then took Hunter to task, "Sirrah, who gave thee leave to read the Bible and expound it?" William gave him the same answer and further said that he resolved to read the Bible wherever he found it, as long as he lived, for that was what the very scriptures enjoined. The vicar got very angry, called him a heretic and to prove it, pressed William to say whether he considered that the bread and wine of the communion, once blessed, became the actual body and blood of Christ. William replied honestly that he considered the bread and wine important tokens, but tokens only, in a service remembering the suffering and death of Jesus Christ, but which could not reproduce His body and blood.

The vicar could not make him change his mind, even though the expression of such ideas was very dangerous, so he told young Hunter that he would report him to the Bishop of London. There is no doubt that he also told the Lord of the Manor, Sir Antony Browne, one of the Queen's Justices, who lived at Weald Hall. Browne knew the family, ordinary hard-working honest folk. He sent for William's father and questioned him about his son's beliefs and his present whereabouts. Mr Hunter could only say that his son had left home, gone he knew not where. But Browne, with all the authority of justiceship behind him, threatened the old man with gaol if the son was not brought before him forthwith. The poor father knew all too well the direction events were now taking. With tears in his eyes he appealed, "Would you have me seek out my son to be burned?" Browne was adamant and so the father had to leave the great house sorrowfully to walk back to Brentwood. It was by chance that he came upon his son, who at once saw how disturbed and apprehensive he was. William listened to his father's tearful account of the interview and the threat of imprisonment. He comforted his father, saying he was ready and willing to submit to Browne's examination and would go along to him at once.

So the formal process of the law was invoked and enforced. On Browne's orders, the village constable put William in the stocks for 24 hours, though at that time he had not been charged with any crime. From the stocks he was taken back to Justice Browne who called for a Bible which he opened at the Book of St.John, Chapter 6. He asked William to give his opinion of the verses relating to the question of transubstantiation, including "... my flesh is meat indeed, and my blood is drink indeed. He that eateth my flesh, and drinketh my blood, dwelleth in me, and I in him" and "... the bread that I will give is my flesh." William could only reply as he had to the vicar, explaining that he could not accept that bread and wine turned into the actual body and blood of Christ at one particular moment in the communion service.

Browne roundly turned on William, telling him he was truly a heretic. He wrote a letter to the Bishop of London, describing the situation and called the constable to take William and the letter down to London. Bishop Bonner read the letter, dismissed the constable and, having William brought before him, said, "I understand, William Hunter, by Mr Browne's letter, that you have had certain communications with the vicar of Welde, about the blessed sacrament of the altar, and that you could not agree, whereupon Mr Browne sent for thee to bring thee to the catholic faith, from which he saith thou are gone. Howbeit, if thou wilt be ruled by me, thou shalt have no harm for anything that thou hast hitherto said or done in this matter." William averred his belief in 'the catholic faith of Christ' with all his heart. The Bishop wanted him then to recant his remarks on transubstantiation, saying: "... I promise thee that thou shalt not be put to open shame: but speak the word here and now between me and thee, and I will promise thee it shall go no further, and thou shalt go home again without any hurt." William replied, "My Lord, if you let me alone, and leave me to my conscience, I will go to my father and dwell with him, or else with my master again, and so, if nobody will disquiet nor trouble my conscience, I will keep my conscience to myself." The bishop was equally careful in his reply: "I am content, so that thou wilt go to the church and go to confession and continue a good catholic Christian."

But William was not prepared to go to church and, by participation, acknowledge the transubstantiation in which he could not believe. He said so, and the Bishop said he would make him. William inflamed him further by saying that the Bishop could do no more than God would permit him. High words and hard words were said, but this was an inconsolable confrontation and so the Bishop was forced to continue William's prosecution. His next step was to put the young man in the stocks in the gatehouse to his palace. He sat there two days and nights, refusing even the crust of bread and cup of water that were the only sustenance offered. The Bishop then ordered his release and said he was to breakfast with his servants. But such was the intensity of religious feeling at the time and such the fear of being branded a heretic that they would not let him sit with them.

Again the Bishop asked William to reconsider his belief in relation to his present dire distress, but he was obdurate. The Bishop, having asked him his age, was driven to say "... you will be burned before you are 20, if you will not yield youself better than you have done yet." He sent him to the prison for common criminals and told the jailer to 'lay as many irons on him as he could bear.' For his subsistence there the Bishop allowed the jailer a halfpenny a day. That cannot have provided adequate food and drink, but it did not break the prisoner's will. For 9 months he languished there, being brought five times before the Bishop and refusing to recant. So he was finally brought before the consistory court of St Paul's on 9th February and condemned as a heretic. His brother, Robert, was in the courtroom and so would have hastened homeward to tell his anxious parents. No doubt the family suffered a good deal of hostility on William's account.

Still the Bishop treated with him, but he could not shake his determined view on that one essential point, so he gave up, saying: "... I see no hope to reclaim thee unto the catholic faith, but thou wilt continue a corrupt member." He pronounced that William should be flung into Newgate Prison until such time as he could be carried to 'Burntwood', there to be burned in public.

When he had dealt with other offenders, he had William brought back and said, "If thou wilt yet recant, I will make thee a free man in the city, and give thee £40 in good money to set thee up in thine occupation; or I will make thee steward of my house, and set thee in office: for I like thee well, thou hast wit enough, and I will prefer thee if thou recant." William replied that if he could not convince him of the rightness before God of transubstantiation, then it was unlikely he would win him over with worldly temptations.

So the die was cast and, after a month in Newgate, William was brought back to Brentwood and lodged in the Swan Inn in close captivity. William's father had said, so innocently, of Newgate, "I was afraid of nothing but that my son would have been killed in the prison by hunger and cold." A much worse death awaited him. The news soon got around and scores of people came to see him, so many of them friends who urged him to believe as he was told, keep his opinion to himself and so save his life.

Three days passed and then the Sheriff, Mr Brocket, came to prepare him for his execution. The Sheriff's son tried to offer words of comfort, but he broke down and wept. William, however, walked staunchly and determinedly through the town, with the Sheriff's man on one side and his brother on the other. His father waited by the way to make his last good-bye, for he could not bear to face the final moment. They came at last to the outskirts of Brentwood, where the butts were set up for archery practice and here the stake had been driven in by the side of the road, though the pile of firewood for the burning had not yet been completed. While he waited William took one of the faggots and, kneeling on it, read the 51st psalm.

Even at this last minute, the sheriff came up to him and said, "Here is a letter from the Queen; if thou wilt recant, thou shalt live; if not, thou shalt be burned." William's answer was, "No!" and he emphasised his decision by going up to the stake and standing against it. Richard Ponde, the bailiff, then came forward and chained him to it. Sir Antony Browne, the Justice who had started the prosecution, complained that there was "not enough wood to burn a leg of him," and when William asked, "Good people, pray for me", Browne growled, "I will pray no more for thee than for a dog." Then William cried out, "Son of God, shine upon me," and the wonder was that at that moment the sun burst out from behind a heavy cloud and shone full in the martyr's face. "I am not afraid," he said as the fire was kindled. Then he lifted his hands to heaven, crying, "Lord, Lord, Lord, receive my spirit." Then, as Foxe puts it, 'casting down his head again into the smothering smoke, he yielded up his life for the truth.' The date was 26th March, 1555.

Was Sir Antony Browne left with a guilty conscience concerning this lad's brave, pointless martyrdom? The question is asked because the record shows that in October, 1557, he bought a piece of land with the intention of providing, in his will, for a school, 'The Grammer School of Antony Browne' to be built upon that site. Perhaps he hoped, by providing education for thousands of boys through hundreds of years, to assuage that guilt in the original reporting for examination one local boy who had the education, the intelligence and the strength of mind to look for what he thought was the truth and to stand by his opinion.

The school continues today, much expanded and with a national reputation, but the chapel wherein William read the Bible that fateful day is now a roofless ruin. It was already being pulled down 20 years after his death. Antony Browne was dead by 1567 and his great-nephew, Wistan Browne, inherited Weald Hall and all its lands. He claimed that the chapel, built about 1221 by David, Abbot of St Osyth, as a chapel-of-ease for the growing population and the constant flow of pilgrims, was his sole property and that he intended to demolish it, using the materials elsewhere on the estate. To this end he had already sent wagons, guarded by men 'sufficiently weaponed' to take away the pulpit and the pews. Next he had the bell and the church clock lowered to the ground and taken away.

Such a sacrilegious act aroused the ire of the townsfolk and brought about what must be one of the earliest 'sit-ins' on record. Let me quote the original indictment in the official language of the court record of 1577. "We, Wistan Browne, esquire, the sheriff, and Henry Grave and James Morice, esquires, justices of the peace, record that on 5th August Thomasine Tyler [and 29 other women, all named], all of Brentwood, were unlawfully assembled in Brentwood Chapel and in the steeple and around the churchyard, and with force and arms they pulled Richard Brooke, schoolmaster, out of the chapel, and beat him, obstructing also the doors of the chapel and locking themselves in, riotously using and bearing against the servants of Wistan Browne and other the King's subjects then present these arms, to wit, pitchforks, bills, a piked staff, two hot spits, three bows and nine arrows, one hatchet, one great hammer, hot water in two kettles, and a great sharp stone; and that they kept themselves in the chapel until they were arrested and removed by us the sherriff and justices on the same day; and that Mary Cocke [and 16 other ladies named] after the arrest escaped, so that they could not be committed to Gaol; and further we record that John Mynto of Brentwood, yeoman, being commanded by James Morice to help in suppressing the riotous persons, refused to do so; and moreover that, whereas we committed Thomasine Tyler to Gaol as a riotous person, Henry Dalley, of Brentwood, labourer, attempted in our presence to rescue her from our custody."

The report is certainly one-sided, compiled as it was by the offender in the case. Reading between the lines, we can appreciate the bravery of these women, who knew they were taking on the might of the local lord and the sheriff to boot. It is comforting to discover that this little 'riot' came to the notice of the Privy Council, no less. They ordered an enquiry and told Browne to cease 'pulling down of the chappell in Burntwood'. They freed all those brave women, ordering only a small fine upon each of them for appearances' sake and they told Browne to explain himself. Despite another attempt at the end of the century to claim possession, our crafty squire was forced to yield ownership of the chapel to the inhabitants at large and its ruins stand today in Brentwood High Street, a monument to women's courage.

Rivenhall sounds like a house that has been split asunder by some natural disaster, but the village actually takes its name, according to Dr Reaney, from two words in Old English meaning 'at the rough nook' - a little place that Saxon settlers may have looked at with despair - so much to do to make it habitable. They did it and that little village persisted through a thousand years to become the commuter's dream of country dwelling it is today.

The old village squire lived at Rivenhall Place for a hundred years from the day in 1692 when Thomas Western, a London merchant, bought the place from the well-known Wiseman family. He died in 1707 and in the next 26 years, the property passed through the hands of no less than five inheritors as death dealt its blows. In 1733 another Thomas Western was installed and he kept health and house until 1766. A subsequent heir, Charles Callis, Baron Western (1767-1844), inherited when he was only 4 years old. He added Felix Hall to the estate in 1795, gathered a wonderful collection of statuary and antiquities there and finally took it as his residence, letting the Place out to tenants. Family tombs in the church of St Mary and All Saints show in their elaborate decoration the importance and the wealth of the Westerns.

The church itself is a thorough-going restoration of 1840, but it stands on the site of a Saxon church whose footings have been revealed in excavations over a 27-year period up to 1977. Interest in the site was inspired by the report of the sexton who, many years before, had reported that a hard pavement limited the depth at which he could dig a grave. The discovery led to the realisation that a large and richly appointed Roman villa was built here, possibly for some great soldier in the occupying army, who commuted to his military business at Colchester. So the very origins of our race and our civilisation can be traced in the confines of a country churchyard and, in this same village, was born a man whose name was noised throughout the land in his own time, a man whose homely words of advice are still quoted.

Thomas Tusser was born in 1524. He is

included in Fuller's **Worthies of England** (1662) and so qualifies officially for recognition as a great man of Essex. He started off, at an early age, as a humble chorister, a young church singer in the service of the King. He came to the notice of influential people and obtained a position as chorister in St Paul's Cathedral, passing from there to the school at Eton and thence to King's College, Cambridge. He later moved to Trinity Hall, and in the company of merry young men spent the happiest days of his life. Though illness forced him to leave, fortune favoured him still, for he found a place at Court as a musician, a 'servant' in the entourage of Baron William Paget of Beaudesert. His appreciation of the appointment is expressed in the dedication of his printed work to his former Lord. For over 10 years in his service Tusser was a contented man, but marriage changed all that.

He left the courtly life to settle with his wife on a farm at Cattiswade in Suffolk. Here it was, after what might be considered only a brief acquaintance with the arts agricultural, that Tusser composed his very long poem setting out the **Hundreth Good Pointes of Husbandrie**, introducing it thus: "In this book who list may look of husbandry and huswifery." That he was an innovator is demonstrated by his introduction of barley as a crop in the locality:

"At Brantham where rye but no barley did grow,
Good barley I had, as many do know;
Five quarters an acre, I truly was paid
For thirty loads muck on each acre so laid..."

His pastoral honeymoon ended all too soon with his wife's illness and subsequent death at Ipswich.

He married again, very quickly, his bride being Amy Moon, 'a wife in youth' whose expensive ways gave Thomas cause for rueful reflection. He had the satisfaction of a wide reputation earned in the publication of his verse and he must have been happy whilst living at West Dereham, Norfolk, under the patronage of Sir Robert Southwell. He had the pleasure, too, of the birth of his children - 3 sons and a daughter. His patron died, his prospects dimmed, another move was necessary, this time to Norwich, where his singing ability secured him the patronage of John Salisbury, Dean of Norwich. His own illness terminated this appointment and brought him back into Essex. He came to Fairstead, where he made a somewhat precarious living by farming the tithes of that parish. This means that he paid an agreed sum to the Rector of Fairstead for the privilege of securing payment in cash or in kind from all the landowners who were obliged to contribute a tenth or a tithe of their profit over a year towards the upkeep of the church. No doubt the Rector was pleased to get a guaranteed sum of money in advance, saving him the difficulties and embarrassments that always attended the gathering in of his rightful dues.

Thomas Tusser experienced these difficulties and was finally overcome by them. He returned to London. The date can be approximated by the entry of the baptism of his third son, Edmond, in the register of St Giles, Cripplegate, on 13th March 1572/3. He may well have hoped for a richer reward in the expansion of his poem from one hundred points to **Five hundreth Pointes of Good Husbandry united to as many of Good Huswifery**, published in 1573. Though he took refuge at Cambridge from the plague in London the following year, he returned as soon as he could, but there was never another upturn in his fortune. He died a miserable debtor, in the prison for such poor unfortunates in the Poultry, Cheapside, on 3rd May 1580. Poor man, he had not made a go of life, certainly not of the farming life, even though his rhymed advice is quoted still. As Fuller said of him, "He spread his bread with all sorts of butter, but none would stick thereon". His epitaph in St Mildred's, Poultry (burnt down in the Great Fire of 1666), is only a little more generous:

"Here Thomas Tusser, clad in earth, doth lie,
Who sometime made the Points of Husbandry;
From him then learn thou may'st, here learn we must,
When all is done, we sleep and turn to dust;
And yet, through Christ, to Heaven we hope to go,
Who reads his books, shall find his faith was so."

Today an author whose book went through at least 9 editions or revisions in his own lifetime is unlikely to gain as little from it as Tusser did. Evidence of the popularity, even today, of his unusual canny verses is shown in the production of **Selections** from our poet in 1954 by the National Federation of Women's Institutes, almost 400 years after the first publication. The preface sums up Tusser's appeal: "The jogging amble of the verse was easy for the unlettered to memorize and his 'wise saws and modern instances' have the authentic ring of experience that the countryman respects."

Tusser assures us of that authenticity:
"By practice and ill speeding
These lessons had their breeding
And not by hearesay or reading."

He tells us of his connection with our county:
"It came to pass that born I was
Of lineage good, of gentle blood,
In Essex layer, in village fair,
That Rivenall hight;
There spend did I my infancy,
There then my name, in honest fame
Remained in sight."

And among those 500 points we should heed for the better husbanding of house and garden, let us read one which is a tribute to Thomas Tusser's gentle nature; and still gives us food for thought:

"What better be than conscience good, to pass the night with sleep?

What better work than daily care fro' sin thyself to keep?

What better thought than think on God, and daily him to serve?

What better gift than to the poor that ready be to sterve?"

Every church in Essex is a history book to those who care to learn the language of architecture, woodwork, sculpture, furniture and the handwriting of its ancient documents and its ever-continuing parish registers. Even when a 'redundant' church has been taken over as a youth hostel, a library, even as a private house, there still persists that atmosphere of prayerful purpose, of people coming together for communal worship and fraternisation through the centuries. One church reflecting this feeling to any person prepared to stop and think for a moment is that dedicated to the Holy Trinity at Colchester.

It boasts the oldest church tower in the town, a rare example of Saxon architecture dated around 1050. The chancel and the south aisle are late 14th Century work, though most of the remainder is a grand restoration and reconstruction of 1886. How could the pious contributors to the great expense have known that before a century had elapsed this church would be unwanted, unattended and turned into a museum of social history? In among the exhibits look for the alabaster monument in what was once the North Chapel. It was removed in that restoration from its important place in the chancel. It was erected there in 1603 and its long inscription in Latin can be roughly translated:

"Ambrose and William Gilberd erected this monument to William Gilberd, senior, Esq., and doctor of physic, in memory of his brotherly affection. He was the eldest son of Jerom Gilberd, Esq., born in the town of Colchester, studied physic at Cambridge, and practised at London more than 30 years, with the greatest applause, and equal success. And being sent for to go to court, he was received into the highest favour by Queen Elizabeth, to whom, as also to her successor, King James, he was principal physician. He wrote a book concerning the magnet, much celebrated by those engaged in things nautical. He died on the last day of November, 1603, in the sixty-third year of his age."

The Treasure of Biography, published in 1866, long before the vast potential of electricity was appreciated, sums up the reasons for this man's fame, which, it says, "rests on his great and original work, entitled **New Physiology of the Magnet, and Magnetic Bodies, and the Earth as a Great Magnet**, which appeared in 1600. It was the fruit of 30 years' labour, and excited the highest admiration among his contemporaries. It is very frequently referred to by Humbolt in his **Kosmos** and is acknowledged to have a character of cosmical grandeur. It is asserted to contain all the fundamental facts of the science so fully examined that little has been added to them..." If that can be said 250 years after Gilberd's thoughts were published, then it must be admitted that he was indeed an extraordinary man. His achievement is further described in the **Scientific and Literary Treasury** also published in 1866, "... electricity can scarcely be considered to have become a distinct branch of science before the commencement of the 17th century, when a book, containing accounts of several electrical experiments, was written by Dr William Gilbert; and it is only since the year 1745, when the properties of the Leyden jar were discovered, that it has made any significant progress..."

Gilberd's direct ancestor, Thomas Gilberd, living at Hintlesham in 1428, was made a free burgess of Colchester. His father, Jerom or Hierom, was similarly honoured in 1553, having settled in the town in 1528. William, in his own time, was famous throughout Europe as a physician and philosopher. He was 17 when he was elected to a fellowship of St John's College, Cambridge, where he graduated in arts and medicine. He then travelled extensively in Europe, as was the fashion for young men in those days. On his return to this country he settled in London and practiced as a physician. By 1599 he reached the very peak of his profession on being elected President of the College of Physicians. It was almost a foregone conclusion that this honour would be followed by his appointment in 1601 as Chief Physician to Queen Elizabeth. She allowed him a special pension in encouragement of his further study and research. That royal appointment continued into James' reign, to be cut short by William's death.

That he became a man of property is evinced by references in Morant's history of Essex to his ownership of 5 properties held of the manor of Elm-

The entrance to 'Tymperleys' on the west side of Trinity Street, where Dr William Gilberd lived

The Gilberd monument in the church of Holy Trinity, now the Museum of Social History, Colchester.

stead and one of the manor of Martell. But when he was in Colchester, he is said to have lived at 'Tymperley's', opposite the church, which has a tablet on its wall in commemoration of the fact that he was born here in May, 1544. William did not marry, so in bachelorhood and with wealth enough to make him independent, he could occupy himself wholeheartedly in his research, working on the manuscript of his famous book during those 30 years. It was published in Latin, the international language of his day, but in 1900 a celebratory English translation was specially commissioned by the Gilbert Club, formed for just this purpose.

Charles E Benham, writing in 1902 **A sketch of his magnetic philosophy**, says of William: "What he laid the foundation of was not so much magnetism or electricity as the way in which magnetics and electrics ought to be studied." His hypothesis was that the Earth is itself a magnet - a great breakthrough in the thinking of the time. It was Lord Rayleigh who said, some 300 years later, "I don't know that we know much more about it now." For nearly 18 years Gilberd experimented and tested his findings again and again, using equipment that would be laughed at by today's laboratory technicians. His careful approach to the subject of magnetism and the qualities and characteristics of the loadstone, cleared away a positive jungle of folklore and superstition which, even then, held the philosophers and scientists in thrall.

The great work consisted of six books in one. The first recounted the history of the discovery of the phenomenon of magnetism down to his own time. The 2nd, 3rd and 4th books considered the qualities of magnetism in attraction, direction, variation and so on, including the important practical aspect of the variation of the compass, and the 5th book covers the 'dip' or inclination of the north-seeking end of a magnetic needle. It had been noticed by others, but it needed William Gilberd to interpret the observation. We can almost be by his side as he discourses upon the value of the compass to the storm-tossed sailor: '... with dark clouds above and around, and no celestial luminaries visible to guide his way...' that

faithful instrument gives the helmsman his exact latitude. 'How agreeable, how helpful, how divine!' exclaims Williams in poetical appreciation. The last book preaches the, then heretical, theory of the daily revolution of the earth. Thus Gilberd became the first reputable English scientist to support this tenet proposed by Copernicus [1473-1543], much to the distress of his friends, for it contravened the canons of religious belief. In Italy, where the influence of the Church was very strong, it is said that many copies of the work still exist in libraries with the last book torn out to protect the morals of the general public. The extent of Gilberd's fame in his own time is shown by the couplet taken from Dryden's epistle, **To my honoured friend Dr Charleton**
"Gilbert shall live till loadstones cease to draw,
Or British fleets the boundless ocean awe..."
Silvanus P Thompson, addressing the Essex Archaeological Society at Colchester in 1903, summed up Dr William Gilberd as '... a man whose true greatness transcends that of Galileo or Bacon, and who is worthy to be set beside Newton or Shakespeare in the memory of his countrymen.'

*John Bastwick - Samuel Purchas
- Mary Honywood - William Kempe -
Peter Chamberlen - William Alexander
- Henry Winstanley*

Gilberd was not afraid to speak his mind on the Copernican theory and risk the consequences, but how many people would be brave enough to stick to their argument and to continue to declare it, even though it meant having both their ears cut off? There was one such man, born in Writtle called John Bastwick. His parents were well enough off to have him educated at Cambridge. Then, after a period of travel and study in Europe, he qualified as a Doctor of Medicine. The physician, in those last days of Elizabeth's reign, was a man feared and respected for his power to heal, so when John took up a practice at Colchester, there is no doubt he would soon have achieved a local reputation.

But he went wrong - he took to writing, and writing about religion at a time when faith and politics were closely intertwined and heads rolled at the utterance of the merest word of criticism. Yet he was determined to express his point of view in print oblivious of the consequences. Our curiosity is further excited by Philip Morant's short account in his history of Colchester published in 1763: '... in a place named the Red-house, formerly lived John Bastwick, Doctor of Physick, who made so much noise in the last century. He was born at Writtle in this county, in the year 1593 and entered into Emmanuel College, Cambridge, the 19th May, 1614; where he continued but a little while. Leaving the University without a degree, he travelled beyond the sea for the space of nine years, where he spent his time between the schools and the camp, and was made Doctor of Physick at Padua. Upon his return to England, he settled in this town, where he practised physick for a while. But some books he published, disagreeable to the Court, brought him into very great troubles.'

There is no doubt that John Bastwick was a good Latin scholar with a talent for expressing himself in print. He could well have had a successful literary career, but he used all that talent to attack what he considered was the flagrant abuse by the Church of its power over the common people. There was more than one reason for a man who liked to see fair play to be angered at the course of events in the first half of the 17th Century. King Charles was anxious to assert his authority and increase his income. One way to achieve the latter was to charge towns on the coast with the provision of a ship for the navy or a payment of a lump sum in lieu. Colchester was required to raise such a sum in 1634 and again in 1635. They managed the first payment, but could not and would not meet the second demand for £400. So there was a good deal of unrest in the town, which would have set a man like Bastwick thinking.

But it was the state of the Church at this time that most upset the worthy doctor and this was the ground on which he conducted his particular, personal battle for fair play for everybody. In the European language of literature and science - Latin - he wrote **Elenchus religionis Papisticae** (Refuation of the Popish faith) and **Flagellum pontificus et epsicoporum Latialium** (Scourge of the high priests and bishops of Rome) and had them printed in Holland in 1633. They consisted of a series of tales of incidents in the lives of English bishops, showing them at their very worst in sins of the flesh and in brutality in their dealings with their flock. Whether the allegations were true or not, one can only say that when the books were read, and Bastwick was inevitably arrested, he must have known that this would be the painful result.

He was brought before the infamous Star Chamber court, that handled cases of such offences as were not provided for under the existing law and gave its own, arbitrary judgement. Bastwick was fined £1,000, excommunicated, and sent to prison with the order that he remain there until he repented and recanted all the charges made in his books, which were all to be burnt. As a doctor he was also 'struck off the register', as we would term it today, but he was made of stern stuff and did not recant. Quite the reverse; whilst in prison he wrote two more tracts, accusing the English bishops of obsequiousness to Rome and inveighing against the tyranny of that very Star Chamber that had imprisoned him. The tracts were published, the Court was apprised and the wretched prisoner was brought before it once again. It declared that, in further punishment, Bastwick was to be put in the pillory in the yard of the Palace of Westminster, that he was to have both his ears cut off, and that he was to be removed to perpetual imprisonment as far away as possible, which meant on the Isles of Scilly.

Yet even here in the courtroom, John Bastwick stood up to his persecutors, crying aloud, "What, will you cut off a true and loyal subject's ears for doing his duty to his King and country? Will you cut off a scholar's ears? Will you cut off a doctor of physic's ears, able to cure lords, peers, kings and emperors? Will you cut off a Christian's ears?... what an age we live in, that we must be thus exposed to the merciless fury of every malignant spirit." His impassioned plea fell on very stony ground, his ears were hacked off and he was bundled off by horse and cart and sailing ship to his island jail.

For 7 years he suffered the conditions of that imprisonment, but, just for once, the story had a happy ending. In 1640, with Parliament in the ascendant, the verdict of that court was set aside. As one historian says, "The doctor's sentence was reversed - save that it was beyond the power of Parliament to restore his ears."! He was released from jail and brought back to London, where a great crowd turned out to welcome him, strewing green boughs and flowers in his path to celebrate his triumphal return. As compensation he was to be paid £5,000 out of the estates of the Church, but they did not give up easily and John Bastwick had to make ends meet by taking up the practice of medicine again, until 1644 when payment was made sufficient to meet the daily needs of his wife and himself.

What adventures, what hardships, what strange lands, what weird experiences! And all set down for us to read by a reverend gentleman sitting in his vicarage of Eastwood in Essex. Samuel Purchas was born at Thaxted in 1577 and educated at St John's College, Cambridge. Having been ordained, he was fortunate enough to be presented to the living at Eastwood by James I in 1604, staying there until 1613. The little Church Guide to St Laurence and All Saints still remembers him, 'the most notable vicar was Samuel Purchas (1604-13). He is distinguished as the second English writer of sea adventure and discoveries. His book in four volumes (1613-25), the first published while at Eastwood, entitled **Purchas his Pilgrimes** was collected from the MSS of Hakluyt and from sailors' stories.'

Though he used other travellers' tales to write his books and find fame, Samuel had his own views on travel, as expressed in his book: 'As for Gentlemen, Travell is accounted an excellent Ornament to them; and therefore many of them coming to their Lands sooner than to their Wits, adventure themselves to see the Fashions of other Countries, where their soules and bodies find temptation to a twofold Whoredom, whence they see the World as Adam had knowledge of good and evil, with the losse or lessening of their estate in the English (and perhaps also in the heavenly) Paradise, and bring home a few smattering termes, flattering garbes, apish cringings, foppish fancies, foolish guises and disguises, the vanities of Neighbour Nations (I name not Naples), without furthering of their knowledge of God, the World, or themselves. I speak not against Travell, so usefull to usefull men.' He was quite frank about his truly vicarious role of teller of tales of travel, saying that it was while still at college that he '... first conceived this travelling genius whereof without travelling he hath travelled ever since.'

He was, said Thomas Wright in 1831, '... a man of universal learning. With great labour and industry, he enlarged and perfected Hackluyt's collection of Voyages and Travels; a work highly esteemed, and valuable for the various instruction and amusement contained in it. He also wrote **Microcosmos, or the History of Man** and other works.' Samuel was fortunate enough to acquire all those stories assembled in manuscript by Richard Hakluyt, who died in 1616, before he could get them published. Hakluyt had, of course, already published his famous **The Principal Navigations, Voyages and Discoveries of the English Nation** and other geographical works. Purchas was happy to acknowledge the great debt he owed to that remarkable man, as we can see from the title page of his book:

HAKLUYTUS POSTUMUS

or

PURCHAS HIS PILGRIMES

Contayning a History of the
World, in Sea Voyages & lande-
Travells, by Englishmen &
others.
Wherein
Gods Wonders in Nature & Pro:
vidence, The Actes, Arts, Varieties
& Vanities of Men, with a word of
the Worlds Rarities, are by a world
of Eywitnesse - Authors, Re:
lated to the World.
Some left written by Mr. Hakluyt at his
death, More since added, His also perused
& perfected. All Examined, abreviated,
Illustrated with Notes, Enlarged with Dis:

courses, Adorned with pictures, and
Expressed in Mapps, In fower
Parts, Each containing five
Bookes.
By Samuel Purchas, B.D.

In addition to these second-hand narratives, there were plenty of opportunities for Samuel to meet those brave seamen, who, sailing out from Leigh, at that time a considerable trading port, could spin a yarn of derring-do in voyages of adventure and exploration. After all, some of them may well have served under Drake's command when he sailed around the world in 1577.

One old salt who provided the vicar with a wonderful story was Andrew Battell. In 1589 he sailed away to the Americas, was captured by Indians and ended up, via Rio de Janeiro, on the west coast of Africa. Through hardships we can hardly imagine, this man endured to see his beloved Leigh again in 1610. What a tale he had to tell! Samuel listened and wrote, and we can read that evocative account today, and feel ourselves by Battell's side as he did, literally, battle on. Another Essex story relates to John Vassal, merchant of London, living in Eastwood, who brought from 'Barbary' - the north coast of Africa - a lion's skin that measured 21 feet from its nose to the tip of its tail.

By the time he had his book ready for publication, Samuel Purchas had moved from Eastwood on appointment as Rector of St Martin Within Ludgate in the City of London, where he was buried in 1626. That church and any monument it might have housed to the memory of Samuel Purchas was completely destroyed in the Great Fire. For all the enjoyment his racy accounts of strange adventures across the seas has given people for nearly 400 years, poor Samuel received less for his book than he paid out to put it together. It is said that in his last years Charles I eased his circumstances by presenting him with a pension derived from the revenues of a deanery. In his will he remembered his birthplace and left five pounds to be distributed among the poor of Thaxted.

The living at Eastwood continued in the

family, for Samuel was succeeded by brother Thomas who officiated until 1657. His resting place is beneath the altar tomb in the churchyard under the east window. The Vassall family, founded in Essex, it seems, by that John already mentioned, lived at Cockethurst Farm, about a quarter of a mile west of the church. It was in 1808 that the last surviving member of that family, Asser Vassall, was buried under the Sanctuary. Samuel Vassall, son of John was, in 1628, granted one tenth of all the land of the new colony on Massachusetts Bay. He never actually went there, but sent his son, John, to further the family fortunes.

From stirring tales of high adventure to the warm security of family life. Dame Mary Honywood came to live in Essex in 1605 when one of her sixteen children, Robert, of Charing in Kent, bought Markshall, Coggeshall, to give more space for his family of fifteen children. Mrs Honywood was married when she was 16 years old. She was 77 when she came to Markshall and she lived there until she was 93.

Markshall, 7 miles east-north-east of Braintree, is the tiniest hamlet imaginable. There is only one road running through it, north to Earls Colne and south to Coggeshall. Fifty years ago the place looked just the same as when old dame Honywood looked out of the window of the big house her son Robert had practically rebuilt and to which he had brought her so proudly. Today, though, a green lawn spreads where once the Honywoods dined in Jacobean jollity. Just such a green and growing carpet cloaks the spot where once rose the church to which the family were brought for baptism and burial. The church, dedicated to St Margaret, was a rebuilding of the early 19th Century, octagonal in shape, red-brick in material, put up at the expense of General Robert Honywood, an indirect descendant from the old family home at Charing.

The Hall and its lands took in nearly all of the Parish itself, thus giving the hamlet its name of Markshall. Now the Honywood sun has set these many years and the land is managed by the Ministry of Agriculture, but the lawns and the lakes, the walks in the woods, seem all too hushed without the background bustle of the big house, the family and the flock of servants. The parish itself has suffered a similar eclipse; its church entirely demolished and carried away, its ecclesiastical needs satisfied by absorption into the parish of Coggeshall.

One problem that the church authorities had at that demolition in 1933 was what to do with the funeral slabs and monuments, especially those to the Honywood family. The answer can be found today in 3 different places. Some were sealed in the buried vaults; the second place is an unlikely spot - directions to it would run: 'Go to Colchester, walk down the hill to Castle Park and through the wrought-iron gates and up the flagged path to the Holly Trees Museum. Do not go in, but turn right and walk round the site to the wooden seat beneath the creeper-covered wall. Among the verdant vines 4 great stone slabs stand against the wall and a modern tablet explains:

The four stones here shown were removed to
Colchester from Markshall Church on its
demolition, March 1933.
1.Robert Honywood 1545 - 1627
eldest of the 367 children of Mary Honywood
whom she had at her decease in 1620 descended
from her. Hhe bought Markshall in 1604.
2.Sir Thomas Honywood 1586 - 1666
his son. Parliamentarian
commander at Siege
of Colchester 1648. M.P. for Essex. Member of
Cromwell's Upper House 1657.
3. Dame Hester Honywood 1607 - 1681
4. Thomas Honywood
Their eldest son, Ob.S.P. [i.e. died without issue] 1672.

But where is the monument to the heroine of our present narrative, old Dame Mary Honywood? At the demolition, her memorial was felt to be too important, too artistic, to be buried or exposed to the wanton damage of weather or vandalism, so it was removed to Coggeshall Church, where it is now set in the wall of the sacristy, teasingly visible over a high screen, but unapproachable through a locked door. This is a pity as it is a beautiful and moving sculpture, in marble, of Mrs Honywood, kneeling in piety. The gilt inscription explains that she was the daughter of Robert Waters of Lenham in Kent, that she married Robert Honywood and was responsible for the astounding number of 367 descendants in her own lifetime and that, as Thomas Wright puts it, 'She led a most pious life, and in a christian manner died at Markshall, in the ninety-third year of her age, the 16th May, 1620.' A further inscription can be translated, 'To the memory of his most dear and pious mother, Robert Honywood, Esq., her eldest son, erected this monument of his duty and esteem.' Mrs Honywood was actually buried beside her husband in Lenham church, so it is a consolation to know that her poor old bones were not disturbed in the great move.

The momory of the good lady lived on, not only in the likeness to be seen on the memorial. Thomas Wright, talking of the house as he saw it around 1830, says that '... in the dining-room there is a fine old portrait of Mrs Mary (Waters) Honeywood in the habit of her widowhood, with a book in her hand: on her hat is inscribed, 'Aetatis suae 70' and on the opposite side, 'Anno Domini 1597'.'

Mrs Honywood was pious, the monument says, but she also suffered periods of most distressing doubt about her faith and her future. 'Religious melancholy' they called it, and it led to the perpetuation of a curious legend long believed in the locality. In her desperate condition she sought the help of many a minister and medical adviser. It was while John Foxe, the famous martyrologist, was trying to console her that, holding a beautiful crystal glass in her hand, she cried, "I am as surely damned as this glass is broken", and dashed it to the floor in her passionate despair. But the glass literally bounced back from the floor and was picked up entirely whole. Apparently the miracle made no difference to her state of mind, though eventually she was able to shake off that religious depression and enjoy once again her true faith and come to comfort others, secure in the love and respect of that amazingly numerous family.

A man who suffered a somewhat similar crisis of self-examination, but with a tragic result, was William Kempe. His family had lived in Spains Hall, Finchingfield, for time out of mind. It may be that it came into their ownership through Nicholas Kempe, who, in the 13th Century, married Margaret, daughter of Richard de Hispania, descendant of the original Norman owners. When William was born there in 1555, to Robert Kempe and his wife, Elizabeth, Spains Hall's west front looked much as we see it today, but then it was entirely surrounded by a moat with a drawbridge on the north side, where the building shows work dated back to around 1480. The splendid chimneys were probably erected in Henry VIII's reign.

William, in his turn, married Philippa Gunter of Aldbury in Hertfordshire in 1588 and one might have thought that their lives would continue in comfortable insignificance. They saw their only daughter, Joan, safely married to John Burgoyne of Sutton, Bedfordshire - and life rolled on. Then one day, in one of those silly rows that spring up between a man and his wife like a thunderstorm in summer, William accused his wife of being unfaithful. He regretted the words almost before they were uttered and must have felt that he should have counted up to ten - and then ten again - before he let fly. He was an honest, worthy man, a man of such character that, feeling that he should make amends, pay penance, he went the whole way, or rather, to the other extreme. Having spoken in haste, he now decided not to speak at all. He made a vow that he would not utter a word to anybody for seven whole years, a self-inflicted punishment. Yet it must have been his wife, Philippa who suffered most from his silence, the very person he first offended!

In the **Essex Review** in 1903, Miss E Vaughan expanded the story, but on what authority cannot be discovered. She tells of William walking, one June day in 1621, in the plantation beside the Hall, full of misery and remorse; of how '... amid the trees, the strong-willed but wrong-headed man registered the dreadful vow that for for the space of 7 years from that day, no word - good or bad - should... pass his lips to any human being. He spoke the words out aloud, and then set his lips into a silence that was never again broken on earth.' But, it seems, there was just one person who overheard him and that was Raven Foster, the local 'cunning man' or white witch, who roamed the woods and meadows in search of the ingredients for is home-brewed potions. He stepped out of the bushes and confronted William; told him no good would come of his oath; said 'sorrow would enter his house'; and other such depressing prognostications. Kempe's oath forbade him to answer, he turned and headed homewards. Since he could no longer speak a word, his family and servants must have assumed with alarm and sorrow, that he had been struck dumb. He could not, would not, explain.

The author continues, 'One interesting feature remains to the present day to show the manner in which the lonely man, shut off from the outer world, sought by a definite work to beguile the tedium of those 7 years. This was the construction each year of a fishpond - or fish 'stew' - each to be stocked with different kinds of fish, and dug one behind the other, till ... seven ponds should remain as a memento of his vow.' But even as she was writing, a curious old map came to light, dated 1618, and drawn up for that William Kempe. It shows the 7 ponds, so they could have been in existence, or entered on the map as contemplated, three years <u>before</u> he made that dreadful vow!

Raven Foster's prophecy of doom if the oath was proceeded with could be said to be reflected in the death of three of William's servants by drowning in 1632 and his wife's death in 1634. Then there was the accident in 1635 when William, riding alone of a June evening, was flung from his horse as it stumbled. He injured his leg and could not get up, yet still his iron will prevailed. He would not call for help, but lay there through the night until his servants came looking for him. He took a long time to recover. Then, in the fifth year of the vow, when he and his groom were riding back from business in a nearby town, possibly Halstead, a wild storm unleashed its fury. They took shelter in an unidentified half-ruined castle; they saw embers in the hearth and William crept up above another room to overhear a gang of robbers drinking and planning another burglary. He was astonished and perturbed to hear his house, Spains Hall, mentioned as the object of their attack. He and his servant stole out of that castle with their hearts in their mouths, glad of the din of the storm covering their retreat, and hastened homewards. But between them and the Hall flowed the Blackwater and the ford was flooded, with only a mile to go. The groom persuaded his master who, after all, could not speak in reply, to take a longer way round by a bridge, while he attempted the crossing with his horse. In haste, William wrote out a note on an odd piece of paper to tell his family to arm themselves, lock all the doors and prepare to repel the robbers; then he set out on the long way round.

The groom got through, but, since William could not speak to him, he could only hand to Philippa the note her husband had written. Unfortunately, the groom's struggle in water and mud had caused the complete obliteration of the writing. The groom could only say that he knew his master was taking the safe, circuitous way, so the family and servants armed themselves - and set out to find him and bring him safely home. While they were away the gang got into the empty house and robbed it. They were never discovered or brought to trial. If William would only have spoken, no doubt descriptions could have been more quickly given and a hue and cry raised at once.

Nobody will ever know whether William Kempe could have spoken again at the end of the term of his penitential silence, because he died even as that period ended. It has been said that he tried to speak, found that he could not utter a sound, and the shock killed him - but we cannot have his word for it! It may be that he had a stroke causing the loss of speech as well as the use of his limbs. So the poor, misguided man died unconsoled and unexplained. His memory is kept green by the monument in the chapel in the south aisle of Finchingfield church, known immemorially as 'Kemp's Chapel'. Part of the inscription runs: 'Here lies William Kemp, Esq., pious, just, hospitable; master of himself so much, that what others scarce doe by force and penalties, he did by a voluntary constancy hold his peace seven years. Who was interred June tenth, 1628, aged seventy-three.'

Take a little Essex village, select one house within it and follow its fortunes through the years. You will unravel in its story the very fabric of the tapestry of our national way of life. Look, for example, at Woodham Mortimer Hall. Its modern conveniences are cloaked by a 17th Century four-gabled facade in warm, red brick. Its white, wooden window frames were once mullioned and transomed of stone in Tudor fashion, and there was a house on this site long before Elizabethan lords and ladies strolled about its gardens. As in so many places in Essex, the church was built in the 7th and 8th centuries, right beside the Saxon chief's 'hall', the better for its protection and the chief's convenience, and Woodham Mortimer has had a succession of halls on this site for all the years of England's history.

Morant, in his **History** of 1768, tells us: 'It is sometimes called Little Woodham. It took the additional name of Mortimer from some of its ancientest possessors.' The Mortimers came over with the Conqueror, but it was Henry II who gave them this lordship. Then Morant described Woodham Mortimer Hall, said to have been built by Sir Cranmer Harris, son of Sir Arthur Harris who died in 1631, for one of his daughters. Peter Chamberlen, a doctor, bought it of the Harris family. He was born 8th May, 1601 and sired 18 sons and daughters. He left behind, in the Hall, an intriguing reminder of his highly original craft, and it was more than 100 years before that reminder, carefully hidden away, was once again brought out into the light of day.

It happened like this: in 1813 a Mrs Kemball, mother of the owner of the Hall at that time, was rummaging about in an attic. She spotted a loose floorboard and noticed that its neighbours were held down by dowels, not nails. When removed they disclosed a secret hidey-hole in which reposed a wooden box 'containing jewels, ladies' gloves, and a few other similar articles,' says the historian writing in 1860. Modesty, perhaps, forbade him to mention the most interesting item of all - some curious tongs. They were shown to Henry Cawardine, a surgeon who had retired to Earls Colne to write a history of surgery, and from his historical and professional knowledge he was able to say that these were the original forceps designed by Peter Chamberlen to ease childbirth, to reduce the loss of babies and of mothers in difficult pregnancies, and by their use to make a very comfortable living.

The sad aspect of Chamberlen's inventive genius is that he kept the miracle-working forceps secret and so did his family for 100 years. From their sole use of the forceps they made much money, but many a mother and child died in the painful process of labour because the medical profession in general could not benefit from the secret instrument. The Chamberlens had come over the sea as religious refugees in Elizabethan times and had established themselves as 'men-midwives' when such doctors were a novelty. William, paterfamilias, lived first at Southampton, then moved to London and its society to further his profession. He had two sons named Peter - a common practice in those days of high infant mortality. It is not clear now which of the three of them was the inventor of the forceps.

The two Peters became members of the Barber Surgeons Company, but in practising their craft fell foul of the College of Physicians by prescribing medicines without authorisation. Peter the Younger married and begat his own son Peter, the hero of our story, who studied hard at Padua, Oxford and Cambridge for his degrees and achieved a Fellowship of the College of Physicians. He then followed his Uncle Peter in being in attendance on King Charles I as Physician Extraordinary, and this before he was 30 years old. The essential ingredient in success with royal and noble confinements was the use of the secret forceps. Then trouble blew up that caused him to lose that useful Fellowship in 1649 and this setback, coupled with the general unrest in London engendered by the approaching Civil War, made him

Woodham Mortimer Hall

see the advantage of a quiet place in the country, not too far from the capital, where he could escape notice yet still carry on his connections and serve richer patients by appointment.

On the accession of Charles II, he was reinstated as court physician, but he still called Woodham Mortimer home. He retired to the Hall in old age and died there in senility. The inscription on his tombstone, including the epitaph he wrote before he lost his mental powers, can still be read in the north-east corner of the churchyard, right next to the garden of his old home:

"Here lyes ye body of Doctor Peter Chamberlen, who was borne ye 8th May, 1601, & dyed on ye 22th of December 1683; being aged 82 years, 7 months, & 14 dayes. He had two wives & by ye first Jane Middleton had 11 sons, & 2 daughters, & amongst them 45 grand Children & 8 great grand Children whereof were living att his death three sons: viz, Hugh, Paul, & John, & his two daughters, and 20 grand Children, and 6 great grand Children. By ye second Anne Harrison had 3 sonnes & 2 daughters; whereof only Hope was living at his Death who hath erected this Monument in Memory of his Father.

The said Peter Chamberlen took ye degree of Doctor in Physik, in severall Universities both att home & abroad, and lived such above three score years, being Physitian in Ordinary to three Kings & Queens of England, viz. King James & Queen Anne; King Charles ye first & Queen Mary; King Charles ye second & Queen Katherine; & also to some forraine Princes; having travelled most partes of Europe, & speaking most of the Languages. As for his Religion was a Christian keeping ye Commandments of God & faith of Jesus, being baptised about ye year 1648, and keeping ye 7th day for ye saboth above 32 years.

To tell his Learning and his Life to men:

Enough is said by here lyes Chamberlen."

There is a further long inscription on the south side of the tomb, all in verse of which a sample is appended, simply because, "These verses were found made written, and ordered by Doctor Peter Chamberlen, here interred, for his Epitaph."

"Death my last sleep, to ease my carefull head,
The grave my hardest, but my easiest bed.
The end of sorrow, labour and of care;
The end of trouble, sickness and of feare.
Here's only to be found, a quiet sleep.
Death's but one night, my life hath many seene;
My life brought death, death brings me life againe.
Seeds rise to trees, herbes rise again from seede
Shall bodies then of men obtaine worse speed.
Wee dayly dye, entomb'd in sleep and night;
Butt in the morning, we renew our light..."

Of his 14 sons, 3 carried on the medical tradition. Hugh was the one who continued in royal service: he even anticipated by 250 years the organisation of our National Health Service with his suggested scheme whereby '...every family might be served much better and cheaper than at present, with Visits, Advice, Medicine, and Surgery.' He it was who eventually tried to sell the secret of his family's success in midwifery. He failed in 1670, when he offered it to Louis XIV's physician for 10,000 crowns, but some 30 years later, he found a Dutch surgeon who saw the value to his practice of those forceps. He bought the secret and, during the 18th Century, the use slowly spread to become standard practice.

It is thought that the forceps found under the floorboards at Woodham Mortimer were, indeed, the original instruments made for the inventive and innovative Peter Chamberlen. The reviewer of Dr Radcliffe's book on **The Secret Instrument** shall have the last word: "The proud position of Essex in pioneering modern midwifery is not generally recognised in the county."

It was Hope Chamberlen who is said to have sold the family house, around 1714, to a Mr William Alexander, who was a London wine merchant remembered by a classic broken-column on a plinth standing in splendid isolation in a field on the other side of the road past the Hall and Church. Despite its age and its exposure to all the winds that blow, the message on its base is still easy to read:

"In grateful remembrance of the munificent bequest by William Alexander Esqr. of his estate at Woodham Mortimer in the County of Essex for the benefit, behoof and advantage of the poor of the Company of Coopers, London, for ever, the master, wardens and court of assistants of the Company have erected this memorial not only as a tribute of their respect and admiration but also with a view of publickly handing down to future ages so splendid an act of disinterested generosity, MDCCCXXV."

High up on the column can be deciphered the coat of arms of the Coopers' Company, including their motto 'Love as brethren.'

Why should William Alexander have made such a generous bequest? The books on the history of the county are unhelpful and it was necessary to go straight to the horse's mouth, as it were, the very Company that commissioned the monument. The Honorary Curator of the Worshipful Company of Coopers has the history of the Company written by Sir William Foster in 1944. Our William was born in or before 1673, son of David Alexander, landlord of an inn in St James' parish, Clerkenwell who was married four times. William is presumed to have been a son of his first marriage to Priscilla. In 1689 he was apprenticed to a cooper, William Phillips, and so the connection with the Company was made. William persevered and completed the 7-year term. In November, 1697, he set up on his own as a cooper, probably of wine casks, and so was admitted to the Livery as a member.

Business prospered, men were employed, trade expanded, and William had money in his pocket. He was prudent, he invested in land, and in November, 1714, he bought the manor of Shenfields, when he was described as a wine merchant. It was a year later that he came to look at Woodham Mortimer Hall in its 300 acres of green and pleasant land. His journey down a mud-mired, rutted lane, besprinkled with horse-dung, in a horse and trap hired from a Chelmsford inn, can hardly be imagined as one stands on the spot today - for the hedgerows have gone, the fields have merged into prairies and the horseless carriages pour past the Hall and Church in a noisy torrent along the smooth, clean tarmacadam. He must have liked the look of it, for he bought it. As far as can be discovered, he did not grace the place with his presence, but leased it out as a farm.

When he died in January, 1726, he was buried at St Mary-at-Hill in London, and his will showed that Richard Carver was tenant at Woodham Mortimer. It cannot now be established whether he was a widower or a bachelor, but one thing is clear, and that is his staunch support of the Coopers' Company, culminating in the evidence of his affection for his brethren as shown in that inscription. There were coopers who had fallen on hard times and were being cared for as pensioners at that time: up to 40 of them. William's magnificent bequest enabled the Coopers materially to increase those pensions. But the value of a bequest of property, particularly farmland, is governed by the demand for it. During the severe agricultural depression towards the end of the 19th Century, the Hall and its land could not be let and the Company had to pay out just to keep it in cultivation. Eventually the depression lifted and the pension fund once again felt the benefit. After further consideration it was decided to dispose of the estate and have the proceeds invested in higher yielding assets. Yet it was not until 1943, with the consent of the Charity Commissioners, that Woodham Mortimer was sold to the sitting tenant.

Sadly, we cannot now see a likeness of our worthy William. The Company decided that a full-length portrait should be commissioned as a token of its pleasure in the bequest. The difficulty was that William was already dead, but as they knew that a portrait was then in existence, they paid an artist named Slack to make a copy of it for a fee of 25 guineas. That was in 1730 and both portraits have now disappeared. However, the Company's gratitude continued on down the years and, almost a century later, their Surveyor, George Smith, was instructed to design that longer-lasting memorial.

Contrast the fury of the Atlantic in a rage with the peace of an Essex church under a steeple soaring above the market town of Saffron Walden - yet there is a connection between the two. Before the striking tower of St Mary's was crowned with this steeple in 1832, it supported a curious 'lantern' made of wood, and local lore has it that Henry Winstanley had it placed there as an experiment in his efforts to provide a life-saving beacon to sailors round our treacherous coasts. Actually it can be seen from old prints of the church that this pleasant idea is no more than folklore, since the lantern was put up long after Winstanley was drowned.

Henry was born in 1644, the first son of Thomas Winstanley of Saffron Walden, formerly of Quendon, who was a mercer of some substance and a churchwarden at St Mary's for four years up to his death in 1680, when he was buried in the South Chapel. Henry's baptism is shown in the Register under 31st March, 1644. It is said that, when he was but a boy, he undertook to repair the church clock and added an ingenious mechanism by which the rising and setting of the sun and moon were shown, represented by two golded spheres, accompanied by a tuneful carillon.

At the age of 21 he was being employed as a 'porter' in the service of James Howard, 3rd Earl of Suffolk, working on the building of the great mansion at Audley End, west of Saffron Walden. When the Earl sold the place to Charles II, Henry passed with it as a servant of the King, to be established there, and at Newmarket, as Clerk of the Works. He showed his skill as an engraver in the production of a set of 24 plans and views of Audley End. One is dated 1678 and the whole set was dedicated to the King, his master, in 1688, and to the Earl of Suffolk and Sir Christopher Wren. As a wealthy man, Winstanley could indulge his passion for invention of 'whimsical mechanisms with which he embellished or encumbered his house.' Alison Barnes, in **Essex Eccentrics**, says they were called Winstanley's Wonders and were shown to the paying public. Examples were a miniature windmill to pump water to the kitchen; a slipper which, when kicked, caused the rising of a 'ghostly apparition'; a trap door that deposited the unwary into the room below; and a chair with arms which tightly gripped the unsuspecting user.

He married Elizabeth Taylor in 1675 and was probably pleased to leave her to demonstrate those mechanical marvels, while he invented and developed what he called a water theatre, sited at the lower end of London's Piccadilly. With much of his money invested in merchant shipping, Henry was very vexed when, in 1695, two of them were lost on the vicious fangs of the Eddystone Reef, off Plymouth. He translated anger into action and planned a method of making sailors aware of the hazard, day and night. It should be remembered that the reef was above water only at low tide and a lighthouse of the type he proposed had never been built before. It was in 1696 that his design was accepted, but it was modified in the building, which started with a solid base 12 feet high and 14 feet in diameter, and was extended to 16 feet in diameter, while the wooden structure rose 80 feet from the rock to the weathervane crowning the elaborately decorated lantern.

But there were perils other than the stormy seas to contend with even before the lighthouse was complete. One day in 1697, a French privateer hove to off the rock, sent a boat and took the builders, along with Henry Winstanley, into custody, while the crew landed on the rock and destroyed every vestige of their work. So notorious were the dreaded reefs of Eddystone and so interested was the Admiralty in the safe-guarding of their shipping that they made special contact with the French government and Winstanley's release was quickly arranged. He went straight back to the supervision of his great design and the lantern first flickered out its warning light on 14th November, 1698.

Subsequently Henry was shocked to discover that, at the height of an Atlantic storm in the winter, the crest of a wave could carry clear across the top of that frivolously fancy weathervane. So, in 1699, he sailed out again with his workmen to take down the complete wooden superstructure, to extend the base to a 24 feet diameter, and to rebuild a tower of stone and wood, rising to a height of one hundred weird and wonderful feet. Derrick Jackson in his **Lighthouses of England and Wales** says, 'It looked like a Chinese pagoda surmounted by a lantern gallery and heavily ornamented with wrought iron.' It cost Henry £8,000, which he was expected to recoup from a charge he was allowed to make on every ship passing his light, according to its size. Quite a sum was needed simply to keep the light going and to effect the constant repairs required after every stormy battering. Having seen so much of the lighthouse in fairer weather when it was a-building, Henry wanted to be in it when one of those storms roared round it. He got his chance on 26th November, 1703, going out to the reef with a repair gang. That night one of the worst storms ever recorded. swept in from the Atlantic across southern England. It blew down 17,000 trees in Kent alone, so you can imagine what went on out in the Atlantic around that fragile, fancy structure with its lamp bravely beaming through the very spray of the wavecrests.

Dawn broke, the tide turned, the wind fell and, when a boat at last arrived off the Eddystone Rocks, its crew was horrified to see the reef quite bare. The whole, wonderful edifice had been wiped off, as if it had never existed. The dreadful fate of Henry Winstanley and his workmen at the height of that storm can be imagined, though it cannot be ascertained.

*James Oglethorpe – Dick Turpin
– Edward Bright – Thomas Plume*

'Cranham, long separated from Upminster by open country, now forms with the latter one aggregate of homes and shops; hedgerows have yielded place to houses.' Not my words, but those of Herbert Tompkins, writing in 1938 his **Companion into Essex.** Yet the church still enjoys a little oasis of peace in the hubbub of the London Borough of Havering, standing as it does at the end of a long drive off the B187. Father Sparling, in the old church guide, sums up the position very neatly: 'The present Parish Church of All Saints and the Hall in the southern part of the parish stand in the Green Belt round London and their rural setting shows what this part of Essex was like in the past. Both Church and Hall have been rebuilt, and imagination is needed to create an accurate picture. Apart from the pasture land and the trees the one feature which is the same is the brick work of the walls both of the churchyard and the garden of Cranham Hall.'

So there has been a lot of change, including the rebuilding of the church in 1874. Yet that is not very evident to our untrained eye, because all the old monuments and memorials were replaced as near as possible to their former positions. Let your attention be drawn to one of those tablets, for it celebrates a man who is remembered in the United States of America with as much gratitude and respect as he is in England. It is placed on the south side of the chancel bearing '... an extravagantly long inscription' according to the **Dictionary of National Biography.** The subject's deeds make him the worthy reason for an entry in that gallery of British 'greats': of him Doctor Samuel Johnson wrote, 'I know of no man whose life would be more interesting. If I were furnished with the materials I would be very glad to write it.' The equally well-known poets Thomson and Pope both made complimentary references to this man. Who was he?

James Edward Oglethorpe, son of Sir Theophilus Oglethorpe of Godalming, Surrey, was born in 1696. Despite his well-to-do birth and upbringing, his sympathy for the poor dictated many of his actions. He was Member of Parliament for Haslemere for 32 years and much of his time in the House was spent in trying to reform prisons and ease the lot of prisoners; particularly was he concerned about the dreadful conditions obtaining in debtors' prisons, where once he had to watch a friend die of the smallpox without being able to help him in his plight. He saw one possible way to help people by the encouragement of colonisation, giving prisoners the chance of a new start in life, in a new country, unfettered by their miserable past. He saw that increased colonisation in America would give rise to increasing trade between the two countries and this was another vital plank in his attack upon poverty.

So it was in a spirit of philanthropy that he led an expedition to Georgia in 1732 and organised the building of the settlement of Savannah. Among his 'First Forty' settlers were many families from the Gravesend area. They explored the Savannah River and, directly through Oglethorpe, made friends with the Creek Indians. In fact, Oglethorpe, himself a General in the British Army, signed a treaty with those Indians and brought back to England one of their great chiefs and his entourage to present him at Court. In the new colony, Oglethorpe laid down laws forbidding slavery, banning the drinking or selling of spiritous liquors and outlawing the exploitation of the Indians. It can be seen how far ahead of his time he was. One American wrote: 'He was the first Englishman who gave America its ideals of non-slavery and temperance.'

He rose to new heights of glory in British estimation when war broke out with Spain in 1739 over 'Jenkins' ear'. The Spanish attacked Georgia, this southern-most colony on the new continent and Oglethorpe, appointed General Officer Commanding the British Forces, knocked them out once and for all at the Battle of the Bloody Marsh. The triumphs and vicissitudes of life in the new colony would need a book to themselves. In its administration Oglethorpe's impetuosity brought clashes with Charles Wesley, who acted as his private secretary and with the Duke of Newcastle, then responsible for the colonies. But that battle had made his reputation and, in 1743, he returned to England as a hero. Through government mismanagement he had to pay most of the cost of defending the colony, practically using up his personal wealth.

Now happened the event that gives Essex the opportunity to claim James Oglethorpe as one of its special heroes. Back in England and 47 years old, he courted and married a much younger woman, Elizabeth Wright, heiress to a considerable fortune on the death of her father, Sir Nathan Wright, in 1727, and her mother in 1741. It included Canewdon Hall and Cranham Hall, where they made their home. Even then Oglethorpe was prepared to return to the colony of which he was still titular Governor and he was busy raising and training a troop of soldiers to take over there, but he was ordered to take an active part in the 1745 rebellion, using those same soldiers. Through some intrigue and, no doubt, a little jealousy of his reputation, he was charged with wasting time in the pursuit of the Jacobite army and had to suffer a Court Martial. Although he he was absolutely acquitted, he knew it meant the end of his career in the army and so he never returned to Georgia, though he remained its Governor until 1752.

He went on sitting in Parliament for a further 2 years, then, when he was defeated in an election, his retirement from public life was complete. For over 30 years he continued a harmonious married life as a country squire, riding out over his estate at Cranham, a much-respected local figure who gathered a circle of 'literati' about him and became a friend of people like Walpole, Goldsmith, Boswell and Burke, 'keeping to the last', as the **Dictionary of National Biography** says, 'his boyish vivacity and diversity of interests, his earnestness of moral conviction.' He died on 1st July, 1785, full of years and honour, a man Essex could certainly be proud of. Thomas Wright, in his history, has it that Oglethorpe was aged no less than 103 when he died, perhaps quoting local rumour, but the fact is that his birth is recorded at St Martin-in-the-Fields in 1696. The rumour may have arisen because that long inscription on the memorial gives everything except his date of birth.

The story does not quite end there. In 1925 Dr Samuel Jacobs of Oglethorpe University at Atlanta, Georgia, got permission from the church authorities to open the family vault at Cranham church and confirmed the presence there of the General's remains. But a request to have them transferred across the Atlantic, to be venerated in the chapel of the University named after him was turned down after reaching national levels. That is why, still today, the little lane sees a steady procession of pilgrims from Georgia coming to pay homage to the founder of their state.

'The transactions of this most notorious offender made a greater noise in the world, at the time they happened, than those of any other malefactor whose life is recorded in the penal collection of this country.' This is the first sentence of a much-battered sixpenny pamphlet on the **Life and Trial of Richard Turpin, a Notorious Highwayman** published in 1808. So, 70 years after he swung on the gibbet, Dick Turpin's exploits were still the subject of much interest and amazement. Though everybody seems to have heard of him, few people realise that he was an

ESSEX PRIDE

Essex man, born and bred. The evidence for it can still be read in the parish register of Hempstead, about 7 miles due east of Saffron Walden. The entry, in Latin, records that Richard, son of John and Mary Turpin, was baptised 21st September, 1705.

Legend has it that Dick Turpin and his mate, Tom King, were honest highwaymen, who robbed only the rich, and on the poor bestowed the blessings of their ill-gotten gains. The romantic view of Turpin's violent attacks and robberies was encouraged in this century by the poet Alfred Noyes in his **The Highwayman** and **Dick Turpin's Ride from London to York**. Even the **London Gazette**, reporting his activities as they happened, says, in its issue of 7th June, 1737, that he was 'The famous highwayman', who 'used the Passengers with a great deal of civility', whilst relieving them of their money. On this occasion he had had the nerve to stop two stage coaches at once, as they came from Saffron Walden and Bishop's Stortford towards London. Turpin had a good enough start in life. His parents kept the Bell Inn, later retitled the Crown, at Hempstead. It seems he had no problems in his young life until he was apprenticed to a butcher at Whitechapel.

This was when the trouble began. It would appear that through '... his parents' improper indulgence in supplying him with money, which enabled him to cut a figure round the town, among the blades of the road and the turf,' Turpin's head was turned. The 'brutality and egregious impropriety of his conduct' in the butcher's home made the butcher discharge him. His friends and family hoped that marriage and a more settled life would draw him away from the evil influences. He was courting a young lady from East Ham, called Hester Palmer, and much to everyone's relief he did marry her and found another job with Farmer Giles of Plaistow. But the improvement in his character did not last long. He lost this job and then, while out of work, stole two oxen from that farmer, drove them to a butcher at Waltham Abbey, where they were slaughtered and skinned. However, Giles' men were hot on his heels; they found the dismembered carcasses, then the skins which were sufficient identification of the stolen property. So they procured a warrant for Turpin's arrest. They arrived at the door of his house in East Ham just as he was slipping out of the back window. Now he was out on his own - a wanted man.

Criminal company was now his only means of support. He joined a gang of smugglers who brought goods from ports like Leigh, at the mouth of the Thames, up the river to London, living the roughest of lives in the shelter provided by the ruins of Hadleigh Castle. This business was not as successful as he would have wished and so he moved across to the Epping area where he found housebreaking, with the aid of one or two cronies, was a profitable affair. The scale of these robberies, and the violence used in them, escalated when he joined more criminals led by a former blacksmith named Gregory. He found a cottage for his wife at Sewardstone and, according to Sir William Addison in his **Essex Worthies**, fashioned a cave for himself and the gang deep in Epping Forest, from which they would sally forth to rob travellers on the London road.

Robbing churches of their valuables was a sideline. In one night the gang rode from Chingford to Barking, breaking into both churches, but being frustrated by the fact that their well-publicised depredations had caused the churchwardens to keep the plate in their own possession for greater safety. Though Turpin escaped capture, other members of the gang were tried and transported, so their operation was broken up completely. It is said that Turpin then retired quietly to Sewardstone and lived there with his wife for close on six months. But one cannot live on air, so it is not surprising to learn that, some time after 1735, he became the ringleader of the Essex gang, specialising in burglary. One story from the pamphlet will serve to show the vicious nature of their attacks.

"Somehow or other Turpin became acquainted with the circumstances of an old woman who lived at Loughton, that kept a great quantity of ready cash by her; whereupon the gang agreed to rob her; and when they came to the door, Wheeler knocked at it; and Turpin, and the rest, forcing their way into the house, blindfolded the eyes of the old woman and her maid, and tied the legs of her son, a well-grown lad, to the bedstead, and proceeded to rob the house; but not at first finding the wished-for booty, they all set about a consultation what to do to get at it; for they were certain that she must have a considerable sum concealed somewhere or other about the house. Turpin began to examine her where her money and effects were hid, telling her at the same time, that he knew she had money, and it was in vain to deny it, for have it they would. The old lady, very loth to part with her money, persisted that she had none, and would not declare anything more of the matter; upon which some of the gang were inclined to believe her, and were sorry for their disappointment; but Turpin as strenuously insisting that she had money as she that she had none, he with horrid oaths and imprecations, swore he would put her on the fire. She continued obstinate for all that, imagining that he only meant to threaten her; and so very fond was she of her darling gold, that she even suffered herself to be served as he had declared, and endured it for some time; till the anguish forced her to make a discovery, which, when she had done, they took her off the grate, and robbed her of all they could find. Some persons talk of a much larger sum, but it is certain that they stole upwards of £400 and decamped safely with their booty."

Success brought confidence. The gang acquired horses and rode out into Kent and Surrey. When robbing the home of a Mr Sheldon at Croydon, Turpin took 11 guineas off the unfortunate man, then returned 2, begging his pardon and wished him goodnight! From such moments of impulsive swagger grew the legend of Turpin, the gentleman highwayman. It was to this occupation that Turpin now turned after the closest of escapes when other members of the gang were captured. With a price of £100 on his head, dead or alive, he guessed it would be safer to operate entirely on his own. He moved off to the Cambridge area and set up with Matthew King already working the area as a highwayman. Turpin took his chance and fell in with him; it gave him a loyal friend and good companion for three years, until King was shot in an attempted hold-up. Some authorities have it that this was when the famous cave was fashioned in the forest, and where, for another three years after his comrade's death, Turpin 'lived, eat, drank, and lay.' The robberies and assaults they committed are too numerous to catalogue.

One day, near his cave, Turpin came upon a couple of men whom he thought were poachers. He advised them that they would not find hares thereabouts. "No," said one man, "but I have found a Turpin", and pointed his gun at him. Turpin kept the man talking while he edged carefully back to the cave, suddenly darted in, seized his carbine, and shot the fellow dead. Now he was in a serious plight. He had to lay low, but he needed money. He hung about the forest and the London road, though he could not keep to his cave which had been ransacked after the murder. Time and again he evaded capture, including an ambush when he thought he had, by mistake, shot his fellow desperado; the incident so tellingly used by Alfred Noyes. He rode away from that encounter, but was further alarmed when he saw afar off, the King's huntsman, Mr Ives, using two dogs on a leash trying to flush him out. It was time to move on.

He kept his freedom for a couple of years, as he moved through Lincolnshire into Yorkshire. Yet still he turned up occasionally in the environs of London and even visited his wife at Sewardstone, drinking freely at the Cock there. From that place he went down to London and made another daring robbery, but being afraid that he had been recognised and pursued, he headed north again and is supposed to have reached York by nightfall of the next day, for he went down to the bowling-green there and took part in a game simply to establish his alibi - for who would believe that it was possible for one horse, and rider for that matter, to cover more than 190 miles in a night and a day?

Here he lived the life of a country gentleman, mixing undetected withh local gentry and farmers. One evening, coming back from a hunting foray, he spotted a cock pheasant in the street. He shot it and his neighbour, one Hall, reported him as a poacher. Before he could make another move, Turpin was

ESSEX PRIDE

arrested. He would not give an undertaking or surety for his future good behaviour and this foolish attitude eventually brought him to book. He was held in the House of Correction at Beverley while further enquiries as to his origin and past conduct were being made. So many claims were made against him, in his assumed name of John Palmer, for horse-stealing and false dealing that he was removed to the prison at York Castle.

After 5 months of incarceration Turpin began to despair. He wrote, in February, 1739, a letter to his brother, begging his help to procure evidence of his good character: "... Few people know me. For Heaven's sake, dear brother, do not neglect me..." But his brother would not pay the postman for the letter. It was returned unopened to the local post office. By the strangest coincidence it was seen by the very schoolmaster who had taught Turpin to read and write and he recognised the handwriting as that of Richard Turpin. The letter was opened and the full import of the discovery was realised. Turpin was brought to trial on two indictments of horse-stealing and the evidence against him was overwhelming. His last pathetic letter was to his father, begging him to get influential local people to intercede for him, so that the death sentence might be commuted to transportation.

Yet, when the time came, he conducted himself bravely enough. The jailers made up to one hundred pounds in showing him to sightseers and in serving him and his friends with the food and drink with which he whiled away his last days. On 7th April, 1739, he was taken in a cart to the place of execution. It was remarkable that, as he mounted the ladder, his right leg trembled, on which he stamped it down with an air and with undaunted courage looked round about him; and, after speaking near half an hour to the topsman, threw himself off the ladder and expired in about 5 minutes.'

Even then his story does not end for his corpse, buried in St George's churchyard, was carried away by body stealers for anatomy. A mob gathered, followed the stealers, and brought the body back through the streets of York in a kind of grisly triumph. It was replaced in the coffin which this time was covered with quicklime.

How times change! A record quoted with amazement by David Coller, the Essex historian, in 1861, does not even get a mention in our modern **Guiness Book of Records.** Coller says, '... Edward Bright, a shopkeeper, was so extremely fat, and of such an uncommon bulk and weight, that there are very few, if any, instances to be found in any country, or upon record in any book. At the age of twelve years and a half he weighed 10 stones and 4 pounds; [increasing] as he grew up, so that in 4 years more he weighed 336 pounds. He went on increasing; and pretty near the same proportion, for the last time he was weighed, which was about 13 months before he died, his net weight was 41 stones and 10 pounds...'

Edward was born on 1st March, 1721, and could claim descent on the maternal side from Jane, sister of Oliver Cromwell. Of his early life not a great deal is known, for his fame for fatness could hardly then have been anticipated. He is said to have started his working life as a postboy on the Maldon to Chelmsford run. Perhaps the riding to and fro in all weathers developed his hearty appetite, but he was only 12 when he gave up that job for an apprenticeship in grocery under a Mr Pattison. He must have had a good head on his shoulders, for by the time he was 22 he had his own grocer's and tallow chandler's shop in Maldon High Street, where Church House is now. A well-stocked shop must have been a great temptation to a large man with an appetite; Edward at this time turned the scales at 30 stone. He needed a good beast to take his weight when he rode to London on business, and his amazing bulk was quite a sight even to the sophisticated citizens of the capital.

It was not long before ever-increasing weight made it difficult and then impossible to mount a horse and walking was reduced to a range equal to the length of the High Street. But Edward did not neglect his business. He could be seen, seated in the doorway of his shop, outside on sunnier days, always

Mr Edward Bright

ready to exchange a cheery greeting with customers and passers-by alike. Now and then he would have a snack, washed down, through the day, with a gallon of beer and half a pint of wine. He was still only 29 when his health began to break up under the strain of sustaining that monumental corpulence. At the end of October he caught typhus, the dreaded 'jail-fever', and died in fever and delerium.

Though there was universal grief at his untimely death, it was mingled with a good deal of curiosity as to how the corpse was to be brought down from the bedroom to the hearse for the funeral procession. No six men could take the weight as bearers of such a massive coffin. The stairs would probably have been unequal to the combined weight, but, in any case, their narrowness ruled out the-possibility. In the event, the bedroom floor was cut away to make a hole large enough to lower the coffin through it to the ground floor and the shop door itself was widened. No wonder a crowd followed the hearse to the churchyard; everyone was wondering how the late, respected Mr Bright was to be interred without dropping the coffin or breaking the backs of the bearers.

In fact, the mournful occasion passed off without incident. but so unusual were the circumstances that the parish clerk especially noted them alongside the entry of Edward Bright's burial in the register of the Church of All Saints, where the hardly-faded writing can be seen to this day, telling the story: "Edward Bright, a tallow chandler and grocer of this town, was buried on the 12th November, 1750, in the parish church of All Saints near the belfry door. He weighed upward of 42 stone (horseman's weight). His coffin was 3ft.6in. over the shoulders, 6ft.7in. long, and 3ft deep. A way was cut through the wall and the staircase to let it down into the shop; it was drawn upon a carriage to the church, slid upon rollers to the vault made of brickwork, and interred by the help of a triangle and pulley. He was 29 years of age the 1st March last, has left a widow now big with her sixth child. He was a very honest tradesman, a facetious companion, comely in his person, affable in his temper, a tender father and a valuable friend."

That is as charming an obituary as anyone could ever hope for. In life Edward Bright was more than a local curiosity; such was his bulk that prints of his portrait were sold throughout the country, often with interesting details appended. They were even translated into European languages and sold on the continent. One print bears the legend: "He was an eminent shopkeeper of that town & supposed to be the largest Man living or perhaps that ever lived in this island; he weighed Six Hundred one Quarter and twenty-one Pounds, computed to be about five Foot nine Inches high, his Body was of an astonishing bulk, & his Legs were as big as a midling Man's Body and though of so great a weight and bulk, surprisingly active.

"N.B. A Wager was proposed between two Gentlemen of that Place & determined December the first 1750, which was that five Men at the age of 21 then resident there could not be button'd within his waistcoat without breaking a stitch or straining a button which when it came to tryal not only ye 5 propos'd but 7 Men were with the greatest ease included."

It is one of those cases where it can truly be said, 'like father like son', for 40 years later in that same burial register there is written, "1790 Edward Bright, tallow chandler and merchant of this town, was buried in the church of All Saints in the family vault near the belfry door 28 March 1790 in the 45th year of his age. He was supposed to be about half the weight of his late father. His coffin was 2 feet nine inches over the shoulder, 6ft.4½in. long and 1ft.11in. deep. He was brought to church on the bier by ten men and interred by the help of triangle and pulleys. He left a widow and nine children. He was a man very much respected by a numerous acquaintance and a valuable friend to Society."

It is a comment on our human weakness to consider that a man should be so well remembered simply for his unfortunate fatness, when men and women whose lives were passed in public service, selfless duty or artistic poverty were forgotten within a few weeks of their demise. At least that same church of All Saints keeps green the memory of some of those people who could have altered the fate and the face of Maldon. To the right of the west door can be seen the figure of St Mellitus, who died in 624 A.D. He was appointed a bishop by St Augustine himself and sent here to preach the new religion to the East Saxons and thus became the first Bishop of London. Then there stands St Cedd, sent here by Oswy about 657 to conclude the work of conversion of those independent East Saxons. He established the little church on the sea wall at Bradwell-juxta-Mare which, after being used as a barn for half a millenium, was in recent years re-consecrated as a monument of our established religion. Further on another postulated likeness stands, that of Bryhtnoth, the ealdorman who led his men into the Battle of Maldon in 991. He exhorted the Saxons to stand firm against the Northmen who had crossed the causeway from Northey Island, where they had set up camp. Such was his courage that he was celebrated in **The Battle of Maldon**, a literary fragment, which, although the original manuscript was lost in a fire, has survived in a transcript as one of the earliest poems in our literary heritage. Bryhtnoth, the poem tells us, was slain in the field by a poisoned spear. A short space, but a long time, separates him from the next figure, Sir Robert Darcy - who gains his place here as High Sheriff of Essex in 1420 and son of a Maldon merchant. He had built the tower now known as the Moot Hall, intending it to be a part of his own house, around 1440. The last figure commemorates Doctor Thomas Plume, who was born here in 1630, and became Vicar of Greenwich and Archdeacon of Rochester. On his death he remembered his home town with affection - and substantial bequests. They included that valuable, not to say priceless, Plume Library, still open to the public, via the old tower of St Peter's, above the present public library. The building containing both libraries was actually built to Plume's orders to serve as a school, in the first instance, and to house his amazing personal collection of books. There are about 5,000 of them, published in the 16th and 17th Centuries, when theology was a subject of the greatest and liveliest interest. Books on astronomy, medicine, mathematics, and history demonstrate Plume's wide-ranging interests. He was a practical man as well, as shown by his bequest of £200 to build a workhouse for the poor and of £1,000 to set up a sack-cloth-making factory to give people employment.

*Samuel Courtauld - Charles Clark
- Frederic Chancellor - Edward Bingham -
Richard Sutton Cheek - The Russian Colony
- John Salter*

Can you imagine a situation today in which grateful workers would club together to pay for a presentation and a dinner at which 1,600 people would sit down in a specially-erected, vast marquee to pay public tribute to their employer? It is not likely that the Chairman of Courtaulds would attract such gratitude today, yet it was the founder of that very firm who was the subject of such a spontaneous demonstration of affectionate loyalty on 26th June, 1846. He was Samuel Courtauld and, still today, thousands of people for miles around Halstead, Braintree and Bocking have reason to thank his enterprise for their continuing employment.

It all started in 1688, when Augustine Courtauld came to England as a Huguenot refugee, a man with the strength of character to flee his country and forsake his established business, rather than be bound by religious precepts in which he could not believe. He simply started all over again in London and saw his son, Augustine, married to Anne Bardin. Of their eight children the youngest, called Samuel, was baptised in the French Church in Orange Street on 13th September, 1720. He was the man who succeeded to his father's flourishing business of goldsmith and made a good marriage with Louisa Ogier, daughter of a French silk weaver who had also settled in London.

Their second son, George, continued the Courtauld line by producing a son called Samuel, after his uncle, George's brother, who had made a successful start in the New World. George followed in his footsteps, arriving in America around 1785, where he met and married a lively young Irishwoman, Ruth Minton. That he counted himself very much an Englishman, despite his immediate ancestry, is shown in a letter written from America in 1793: "May God bless old England. In a political sense she is corrupt, but I love her private character, and her manners are congenial to my own." Very shortly afterwards, on 1st June of the same year, George's third son was born in Albany in the State of New York. He was christened Samuel. Fortunately for England and for Essex, this young Samuel, just a year old, came back to 'old England' with his parents, when his father entered into partnership with a man named Noailles in the manufacture of silk.

Though they lived at first at Sevenoaks, they moved in 1798 to Pebmarsh in our county when the partnership was dissolved. There, in conjunction with a Mr Witts, he set another silk-weaving factory in motion: "Building", as his daughter recollected in 1896, "factory, dwelling-houses, and cottages for work-people, and turning a wilderness into a scene of tasteful comfort and extended usefulness." So Courtaulds first came to Essex, and the experiment was so successful that George went into the business on a much larger scale. He partnered Joseph Wilson of Highbury, London, in a brand-new silk factory at Braintree which he again saw through from the laying of the first brick. All that hard work was wasted, however, because the partners fell out, and there was much time and money spent on litigation before the final dissolution in 1817. D C Coleman, in his **Courtaulds**, sums up neatly, "The dispute ended George I's business career, but it started the much more important one of his son."

George went back to America, working with

his father in a scheme to buy up land not yet settled, near Marietta, Ohio, and to set up a society of workers and capitalists to develop it to their mutual advantage. But it caused them great hardship and suffering, culminating in George's death from the ague and yellow fever in 1823. Meanwhile, his son, Samuel, had stayed in England and ventured into business on his own account, setting up a mill in Panfield Lane in 1816. The following year his cousin, Peter Taylor, was persuaded to throw in his lot with him and a new, bigger site was looked for. Within a year they had found land at Braintree for a factory large enough to treble their business and had the mill built within the year.

But there were many problems, not least of which was a developing antipathy between the partners. Business declined and Samuel had to think hard about the way ahead. Peter Taylor was dropped as an active partner, the Panfield Lane factory was given up and the New Mills at Braintree were sold altogether, while Samuel secured the lease with option to purchase of the water-powered fulling mill at Bocking, formerly run by the Savills. Much of the money that kept him afloat at this time was lent by his good friend John Newberry and some came from family funds that had to be repaid. Through hard work and hopefulness, business picked up. By 1822, Samuel was able to record that he was making £1,000 a year. One great contribution to that success was his introduction of the manufacture of crape.

For a definition of that term, Samuel Maunder's **Scientific and Literary Treasury** of 1866, describes it as 'a light transparent stuff, resembling gauze. It is made of silk, gummed and twisted in the mill, and is much used in mourning.' The Victorian penchant for deep mourning and conventional dress for the purpose made crape much in demand over a long period. So the business was soundly based and Samuel's total dedication to the job, his tremendous capacity for work and his ability to get the best out of other people, made the firm's future rosy indeed.

A new development in 1825 was the conversion of the corn-mill, called Town Mill, in Halstead, to make crape on contract. More buildings were erected at the Panfield Lane site, a small steam engine was installed at the Bocking works and, one way and another, Samuel was able to take into the business those relations who had recently returned, rather chastened, from America. This building and enlarging was good news for local folk out of a job in the agricultural depression, for the work force was quickly doubled. What is more, in the words of C Fell Smith in the **Essex Review**, "Both Mr and Mrs Courtauld looked personally after the welfare of their workpeople, and were untiring in their efforts for the education, amusement, sustenance, and good housing of every man, woman or child whom they employed." Concerning his great interest in housing his workers satisfactorily, Samuel Courtauld half-humorously remarked, "When I die, I should like to have written on my tomb, 'He built good cottages'." It was not, but he certainly did.

The very real love and respect felt for their employer and his wife is proved by the most unusual dinner given in their honour and paid for by the workers at the 3 mills, and celebrated further by the striking of a special silver medal to be presented to them and to other members of the firm. A description of the medal gives a clear picture of the thought behind the occasion. On one side is inscribed the arms of the Weavers' Company accompanied by their motto 'Weave truth with trust', and supported by two banners below on either side of a beehive, proclaiming 'Honour to whom honour is due' and 'Blessed is he that considereth the poor'. All around the circumference the message runs, 'Wealth, talent, labour, each respecting all; united prosper, but divided fall.' The other side has 3 banners around a cornucopia, reciting, 'Long live the Company' and 'By winders aid our wealth is made', while all around the message runs, 'Dinner given to Samuel Courtauld, Taylors and Courtauld, by 1,600 of their people. June 26, 1846.'

All these people sat down together in a vast marquee erected in a field next to the Courtauld family home, the Folly at High Garrett, Bocking Street. Such now was the influence of the Courtaulds in the area that the townships of Braintree, Bocking and Halstead declared, to all intents and purposes, a public holiday.

Crowds of workers in procession from each place came together at High Garrett and formed a crocodile, 4 abreast and a mile long. It was such a sight that it drew further crowds of spectators. It was estimated that 5,000 people flocked into that field. The main address at the dinner extolled the qualities of their principal employer, "Your own honourable conduct, your love of, and strict adherence to principle, have not a little tended to raise those around you in the moral and social scale, while the patient and persevering manner in which you have attended to the complaints of the smallest child in your establishment has inspired a confidence in your justice not often equalled, and exhibited you as the father rather than the master of those over whom you preside.

"May you long be spared still to improve us by your example, and to promote our interests by your considerate care, and when time, who has placed his hoary honours on your head, shall summon you to another and better world, may your exit from this be as peaceful as your part here has been honourably sustained."

Samuel's reply gives a glimpse of his character: "Yes, I do know what it is to eat bread earned by the sweat of a man's brow; and all my sympathies and all my feelings of fellowship are with those who honestly and nobly earn the bread they eat by work... I dwelt with more and more true satisfaction on the increasing number of workpeople to whom we were able from time to time to give employment..." As D C Coleman says, "To a very substantial extent Sam Courtauld was the firm which bore his name. He made it, shaped it, ran it, dominated it. Even in the later years of his life, when no longer an active partner, he did not hesitate to make his opinions felt on a variety of questions..." Even when he was 87, he still told the tale that when someone asked him, when he was a little boy, what he would like to be when he grew up, he said, "Anything - in a large way." He was a paternal employer who successfully strode across the wide gap between the small business he started in the old and now-demolished Panfield Lane mill and the great establishment of the world's leading crape manufactory, into which it developed, inspiring all who came under his influence and carrying all before him with drive and determination.

He had married Ellen Taylor and they lived together in happy harmony for nearly 50 years, until she died in 1872. Surely the great tragedy of Samuel's life, and Essex life thereafter, was that they had but one child, born in 1840, which only lived to be just one year old. They will long be remembered in Gosfield, for, from about 1854, they made their home in Gosfield Hall and, after his wife's death, he lived on there in splendid isolation, supported by his adopted daughter, but entertaining very little. Increasing deafness prevented further activity in public life, but he still showed a great interest in the business and would have been so proud and delighted if only he could have lived on to 1886 when, at the high point of the firm's expansion, it was employing 3,214 people, one of the largest work forces in Essex at that time. As to Gosfield, it has been said that in his determination to beautify its environment and with his customary generosity, he transformed the whole village, building model cottages, paying for the erection and equipment of the new school and founding a village club and reading room.

So the grand old man continued his life among his workmen, ever respected and admired, not least for the business acumen that had guaranteed happy employment for so many Essex people. He died on 21st March, 1881, and was buried at Gosfield. The Courtauld family down the years reflected Samuel's interest in people and his generosity. The splendidly decorated Braintree Town Hall was built and furnished at the sole expense of Sir William Julien Courtauld in 1938. Another Samuel became Chairman of the Board and an ackowledged connoisseur and patron of the arts. He endowed the world-famous Courtauld Institute of Art, while, back in Braintree, the hospital, the church, the Institute building, the Museum, the Village Hall, the Public Gardens and the

Recreation Ground have all been financed in one way or another by this most beneficent and benevolent family of local employers. Old Sam would have been proud of them.

Essex is not so much proud of Charles Clark as puzzled by him. From what can be construed today of his life in the first half of the 19th Century, he must be accepted as an eccentric. He first came to public notice in 1830, when as the son of a tenant farmer at Great Totham and a keen amateur printer, he combined with his friend and neighbour, George W Johnson, in the writing, setting up, printing and publishing of a history of Great Totham. Charles was born in Heybridge in 1806 and returned there in his retirement. He was educated, "... for the most part at Witham Place School... run by the Rev. J S Dunn..." - one of the few clues he gave in his publications to his early life. It would appear that he was the son of a farmer, in whose occupation he followed.

It was in 1823 that his father, Robert, took over from Isaac Poole the tenancy of Great Totham Hall and the farm that went with it. By the time he was 19, Charles had composed a number of verses, demonstrating what was to be his life-long interest and pastime. One of these verses, **Sylvan Scenes**, was eventually published. It was as a young man of 24, having acquired a small printing press and taught himself how to operate it, that Charles Clark offered to undertake for his friend the printing of the 72-page **A History, Antiquarian and Statistical, of the Parish of Great Totham**, which he claimed to have produced at his sole expense. The experience gave him confidence to publish his own compositions, mostly in verse, and all abounding in atrocious puns and tricks with words which point up that eccentricity that was already beginning to set him apart.

The one firmly-held belief of his life, the essential necessity in this country of birth control, is summed up neatly in Sir William Addison's evaluation of the man in his **Essex Worthies** - "His fanatical advocacy of Malthusian principles coupled with his personal oddities, made him a noted eccentric, whose works came to be collected as curiosities." Malthus was the author of the **Essay on the Principle of Population** (1798) that gave rise to much discussion and not a little hostility towards the author for his proposition that world population was running out of check and needed a determined action to bring it into bounds.

As a bachelor, Clark was in a more favourable position than most to practice birth control and, under that Malthusian influence he composed a new version of the National Anthem, pleading for a stop to Queen Victoria's continuing production of children. He printed and published it as a broadside, signed 'Doggrel Drydog, Tiptree Heath, 1843'.

GOD STOP THE QUEEN!
a new version of
The National Anthem

God stop quick VIC our Queen!
O! thwart our fruitful Queen-
God stop the Queen!
Make her notorious
For deeds <u>somewhat</u> glorious,
And AL. less uxorious -
God stop the Queen!

O! sages near, arise!
At once with her advise,
And make her hold:
Condemn that work of VIC.'s -
Frustrate her bearing tricks;
On us <u>a score</u> she'll fix -
O! save our gold!

Her dreaded group in store,
On us ne'er may she pour;
Long let her rest.
May she grow wise and pause,
And give us much less cause
To pray - with famish'd jaws -
GOD STOP THE QUEEN!!

An extreme example of the fascination alliteration had for him is the title-page to the collection of excerpts from many different authors that he assembled, printed and published, on the inadvisability of marriage and the problems following in the train of procreation. His title runs **Mirth and Mocking on Sinner-Stocking, Pickings and Pleasantries for pothering and pauperizing populators, presenting a peculiar, persuasive, and profitable profusion of pages, portions and pieces in poetry and prose...** After 60 words, this becomes trying and affected. Affectation could also be the criticism levelled at Clark's unusual poetical innovation - verses rhyming both at the beginning and the end of each line. He was modest enough about his versifying, saying in a letter to John Clare in 1832, "... I have never dared to publish anything except in periodicals."

In maturity he was an obsessive letter-to-the-press writer with contributions published in papers like the **Family Herald** and the **Chelmsford Chronicle**, on a wide variety of subjects and offering advice in verse on the local and political events of the day. He found another, quite delightful method of broadcasting his metric messages; he used small gas-inflated balloons, to which he tied his verses, entitling them **The Balloon, to its Finder** and sent them off to an unknown audience, selected entirely at the whim of the wind. An instance of Clark's sense of humour is the little verse he penned when in the severe winter of 1837, someone stole a sheep from his farm:

"The sheep-stealing case, at Mr Clark's,
Is vexatious altogether;
Instead of the <u>ewe</u>, the scamp, just now,
Should have taken away the WEATHER!"

His advocacy of birth control was the spur to the production of his most ambitious and most considerable work, with that mysterious title of **Mirth and Mocking on Sinner-Stocking** - meaning, simply, a collection of comments from a hundred and one sources on the disaster of marriage and the penalties of parenthood. It was published as a book, edited by W L Hanchant, in 1932, together with some letters between Clark and the poet John Clare, as well as verse printed as broadsides by the author. "**Mirth and Mocking...**" says Henchant, "was never to be published as announced; the book now presented under

ESSEX PRIDE

that title only collects together the specimen 'pickings and pleasantries' displayed on the four announcements... shorn of the promised 'appendix of curious cases', that History traces..."

While he farmed the land and printed his books and wrote his letters to the press, Charles Clark reserved a little of the midnight oil for another passionate interest; that of getting together a library of old books and pamphlets, more particularly on East Anglia. No doubt the old ballads and folk tales that he sedulously gathered were a guide and inspiration to his own versifying.

Because so much was of purely local interest, often penned to amuse friends rather than for publication, Charles Clark has been dismissed as a poet. His obsession with birth control also went against him, yet in **John Noakes and Mary Styles; or, an Essex Calf's Visit to Tiptree Races**, published by London publisher, John Russell Smith, in 1839, he makes a serious contribution to dialect poetry, summed up by John Hallamby,

John Noakes and Mary Styles will long be read, -

And will to ages yet unborn transmit,
In purity, the Essex Dialect."

On that small printing press of his and, no doubt, by the light of an oil lamp on a winter's night (for a farmer could not spare the daylight hours), Charles Clark set up valuable reprints of old pamphlets and local books in his collection. For example, he reprinted Thomas Tusser's **A Hundreth Good Poyntes of Husbandrie**, Matthew Hopkins' (the witchfinder's) **The discovery of Witches** of 1647; and Sir Egerton Brydges' **Human Fate**, actually printed from the author's manuscript in 1846.

By about 1853, Charles gave up farming and went back to his native village of Heybridge. It is likely that it was at this time that he sold his extensive library. By 1860 he was living in quiet retirement. In 1875 his neighbour, Cornelius Walford, described him as '... a plain, simple-minded man to all appearance, one of the type who never seem to grow any older.' He died in March, 1880, at the age of 74. Georgina Dawson sums up his contribution to

Essex life in an article in the **Essex Review**, "In his own age a noted eccentric and 'character', but condemned and forgotten by the following generation, Charles Clark was one of the first to reprint original texts of local interest with care and accuracy, and to preserve for us some of the foibles of his own times.'

If anyone could be said to be First Citizen of the county town of Chelmsford, the honour would surely fall to Frederic Chancellor. He was, after all, the first Mayor Chelmsford ever had, being elected in 1888, when the town obtained its Charter as a Borough with its own council. Chancellor played many parts in town and county life for more than 70 years, even though he did not arrive in Chelmsford until he was 21. A Londoner by birth, who had served his articles in architecture, Frederic came to Chelmsford to join the firm of James Beadel & Son. Three years later he was taken in as a partner and his name went on the brass plate outside the office.

That was in 1849. The same year this young man became the first person in Chelmsford to organise a 'dig' and publish a report. Chancellor set out his findings in the **Transactions** of the Essex Archaeological Society, concerning the excavation of Roman remains found off Mildmay Road on the Moulsham side of the town. Naturally, the report was supported with well-drawn plans, as befitted an up-and-coming architect. He was one of the founder-members of that Archaeological Society, based in Colchester, which continues a lively existence.

At this time local goverment was slowly on the change, forced by increasing population in a growing number of towns, a totally inadequate water supply and a long roll of death from infectious illnesses. Local Boards of Health were set up to put matters right and, in Chelmsford, Frederic Chancellor was considered a fit person to be elected, though he was but 27 years old. He remained to shape and influence Chelmsford's government for 65 years.

Architecture was his profession, however, and Beadel, Son and Chancellor produced a considerable volume of work. For example, Chancellor designed the recently-demolished Corn Exchange standing in Tindal Square in 1857. Two years later he was Number One again in Chelmsford when he was the first to join the Chelmsford Volunteers and was entered as Number One on the muster roll. He must have been a model recruit, for he rose right through the ranks to retire, in 1888, as Lieutenant Colonel and Commandant of the 2nd Volunteer Battalion of the Essex Regiment. In 1860, after the death of his senior partner, he set up his own offices in Chelmsford and London.

His considerable output of work increased still further from 1871, when he was appointed surveyor to the diocese of St Albans, which then embraced Essex. It meant that he had a hand in the designing, restoration and repair of churches all over the county, so he can truly be said to have made a lasting and very visible contribution to the architecture of Chelmsford and Essex. He was able to combine his professional and pastime interests in the preparation of notes on churches and other buildings to be visited by the Essex Archaeological Society.

All the while, too, he was collecting information, detailed measurements and drawings on and of the ancient sepulchral monuments still existing in Essex churches.

His son, Wykeham, following in his architectural foot steps, provided the illustrations for a huge book that Frederic had published in 1890. Once again, his uniqueness established itself, for this book remains the biggest kept in the Chelmsford Library's local history collection! He had other literary interests in that he was a Trustee of the Knightbridge Library, a collection of religious books left to the town in 1679 by Dr John Knightbridge, which was revived in 1903 and placed in the room above the south porch of Chelmsford Parish Church, the restoration of which was at Chancellor's own expense and, of course, to his design.

He had continued his association with the Local Board of Health, being the Chairman when moves were afoot to apply for a Charter of Incorporation as a Borough. This was in 1888, when Chancellor was 63. Understandably, he was in favour of the status quo and worked against such incorporation. He lost the day, however, but such was the respect in which he was held that, when the Charter finally gave Chelmsford Borough status, it was Frederic who was asked to become the first Mayor and willingly he did this, saying: "If the majority of the inhabitants could satisfy the Privy Council that Chelmsford was entitled to a Corporation as the most desireable form of government, so be it." It was noted in the local newspaper that on the day of the reception of the Charter, Mr F Chancellor's house 'took the cake' for the originality and artistry of its decoration to celebrate the occasion, 'although Mr G Bolingbroke's and Mr E Durrant's were a very good equal second.'

Fred Chancellor's ability to change with the times, is demonstrated by that appointment as Chelmsford's first Mayor; in 1891 he was elected an Alderman and also appointed a Justice of the Peace, holding both offices until his death. By 1906, when he was 81, he had been elected Mayor 7 separate times. This amazing record of public service was crowned by the opening in the same year of the public library. Though the building was paid for by Carnegie, Chancellor had worked hard for years for its establishment and in the interests of better facilities for self-education.

At the age of 82 he took his place on the newly-formed County Council for the first time and served on the Chelmsford and District sub-committee of the Education Committee. He carried on his service to his community for a further 10 years and his lively mind found expression in his interest in archaeology and local history in articles written for the **Transactions** of the Essex Archaeological Society and for the **Essex Review** from its inception in 1892 to the year of his death. It was in the latter periodical that he had published the tables of statistics of rainfall from daily records he kept over 34 years. At last his great age and growing infirmity began to tell on him and Frederic decided that the time had come for retirement from County and Borough Councils.

He called it a day in the autumn of 1917 and the Borough Council convened a special meeting to move, with acclamation, that Chelmsford should confer upon its leading citizen the highest honour in its power, the Freedom of the Borough. He was not well enough to attend a ceremony in the Council chamber, so a deputation called on him at home to make the presentation of the Freedom as set out on vellum, sealed with the Borough seal and contained in a silver gilt casket. This was one rare occasion when Frederic was not first, but second; the first Freeman was Field Marshal Sir Evelyn Wood, enrolled in 1903. Frederic, on signing the Roll of Freemen, humorously commented that as the Borough's youngest (most recently elected) freeman he would have to write to his elder brother and ask if there was anything he could do to take care of him. In age, of course, Sir Evelyn was considerably younger.

It must have been an effort for Frederic Chancellor to make polite conversation at this time, for he was a very sick man. Within two months, in January, 1918, he was dead. Reminders today of that long life of work for Chelmsford are the memorial oak screen in the Cathedral, designed by Wykeham; the Frederic Chancellor scholarship, set up by public subscription that still helps a Chelmsford student going on to further education; and the naming of Chelmsford's biggest public hall, opened in 1972 by his grand-daughter, Margaret Wardrop, as the Chancellor Hall. An extensive collection of his architectural drawings was rescued in the clearing out of an architect's office recently and was passed to the Essex Record Office.

Edward Bingham was an unusual Essex potter. His work is so unique that it is instantly identifiable and though not easily found today, it can still be collected without great expense. Much is represented in Essex museums, where the would-be collector can study it at his leisure. Certainly his work is of the class of which one could say increasing familiarity brings deeper appreciation. Edward owed his skill to his father, also Edward, who started the family business. He came from Blackheath to Gestingthorpe, where he set up a pottery producing earthenware plant and garden pottery. At times he aspired to decorative urns and included such trifles as puzzle-jugs.

Our Edward was born in Blackheath in 1829. He was 8 when his father moved from Gestingthorpe and set up his own pottery beside a small cottage standing literally in the shadow of the great Norman keep at Castle Hedingham. Here he continued his productions in plain, honest-to-goodness earthenware. So young Edward grew up playing with clay, as we might play with plasticine. From that early age he had shown an interest in modelling clay and in wood-carving, copying the natural objects he could so easily find all about deep in the Essex countryside - flowers, insects, snakes. The vicar encouraged this bent by lending books with helpful pictures.

Information on his youth is scanty. We know he went to Rugby, acting as an assistant to an uncle who ran a school for deaf and dumb boys and picking up, in the process, a smattering of Greek and Latin. That was a passing phase and Edward returned home to help in the pottery and to produce his own individual pieces, glazed, with a profusion of coloured and moulded decoration. They occasionally found a buyer amongst those who came to purchase the plain ware associated with Bingham Senior. Edward had to take over from his ageing father and he had to take on other work to keep the family's heads above water. The 1851 Census shows that he was then running a boys' school; later he obtained a subpostmastership.

Business was brightening, however, and the Factories Act returns of 1864 show that he was employing a few people at the pottery. According to Edward himself, 1874 was a turning point in the improvement of his pottery and his profits. It was then that he read Meteyard's **Life of Wedgwood** and determined to improve the quality of his own wares. The new products in their pleasing blues, greens and browns, and highly decorated, were now being bought by wholesalers from counties bordering Essex. The seal of approval was stamped upon his work by the visit of the Royal Archaeological Society to Hedingham Castle in 1876. The members could not help noticing the strange little pottery tucked away by the humble cottage. They looked over it, admired Edward's efforts and bought many pieces. He came to the notice of the local cognoscenti, was 'taken up', and so Edward reached his golden age. In 1885 thirteen kilns were in operation.

In the following year Castle Hedingham pottery was granted the accolade of approval by the **Essex County Chronicle** which sent a reporter into the wilds of Essex to investigate this new-found manifestation of art in the area. "Having determined to give the worthy proprietor a call and inspect the work carried on in this old-world little pottery, we enter the little gate in the lane near the Vicarage and are immediately confronted by a small glass-fronted show case in which are a few specimens of the articles produced in the works..." The reporter ambles on to the pottery shed, "The walls... and the beams seem every inch of them to be covered with texts of scripture having reference to potters and pottery, and roughly written in chalk or on slips of paper; with sketches embracing specimens of pottery of all times and kinds... At a wheel near the entrance sits Mr Edward W Bingham, the eldest son of the proprietor, who seems to have developed a natural aptitude for the finer and more artistic pottery work..."

The writer noted copies of classical and mediaeval pieces, as well as Edward's highly original products. The one outstanding item, so typically 'Hedingham Ware', was the 'Historical Essex Jug', showing us Edward's natural curiosity, his interest in history and his pleasure in passing on knowledge he had gained. What is more, this jug, repeated in only in a limited number, shows his skill in added decoration. When, in recent years, one of these delightful jugs was bought in a secondhand shop, a tightly folded piece of paper was found pushed down into the neck. Rescued, dusted and unfolded, it was found to be a description in Bingham's own hand of all the signs and symbols used in the decoration, written out for the original purchaser:

"Centre medallions: Essex displaying her resources to curiosity and agriculture. The two side medallions shew an Essex victory by Boadicea over the Roman Legions at Messing and the 2nd the Dunmow Flitch in ancient times with a procession of 'Essex Calves'. Around these are depicted Hops and

Safferon with Essex Wheat on the Brim and Native Oysters down the handle. The arms of Essex boroughs around the neck are those of Chelmsford, Colchester, etc. The other shields are those of ancient Essex families De Vere, Symonds, Tyrell, Bourshire, Mildmay, Chapels, ancient County Buildings appear around and about the jug as Colchester, Hadleigh, Saff-Walden, Hedingham Castle, Beckenham Gate, Waltham Abbey, Tilbury Fort, Layer Marney Gate Tower. The very ancient coinage is represented by coins (obverse & reverse) of Cunobelin, Constantinus and Carausius. The arms of Essex surmount the handle.

 Designers and Ecuters. & Modrs.
  E.Bingham and E.W.Bingham
   Pottery
  Castle Hedingham
  Essex."

 The first trial piece for the production of this jug was most fortunately preserved and can now be seen in the Chelmsford and Essex Museum. Bingham's flights of fancy in pretty decoration, and his careful attention to detail in exact reproduction of the coats of arms are clearly seen in this one work of art.

 His ambition, even as a village potter, can best be judged by two other examples. The first is the De Vere plaque, all of one and a half inches thick and thirty inches in diameter, made from local clay, probably dug out by the potter himself. It is most profusely decorated with separately made ornaments and coats of arms copied from the tomb of John de Vere, 13th Earl of Oxford, who was buried in Castle Hedingham church in 1539. The second is Edward's largest work, $37\frac{1}{2}$ inches high, a copy as exact as he could make it, of the famed Porsena vase that he made for Lady Margaret Majendie and which was, apparently, later owned by Mr Samuel Courtauld.

 Our potter's sense of humour is evident in the many puzzle-jugs he made. They were at one time popular in the pub, good for a laugh when an unsuspecting stranger tried to pour his ale. So many spouts – which was the effective one? The only way to get a drink was to stop up all the spouts but one and then suck at that. One such jug is inscribed with the vague clue: "Cork tight below - Fill me full - Find how I go - Take a pull." Another hardly-amusing series of mugs has a toad modelled in the bottom, looking up at the drinker who only sees it as his ale is supped. In 1894 Edward achieved the satisfaction and the honour of exhibition at the Home Art and Industries Exhibition at the Albert Hall.

He was 75 then, yet he kept the pottery going until 1899, when his son took over. He did not have his father's passionate interest in the work, but was content to live modestly, letting traders come to him for his wares and, when business declined, he sold out to the firm that supplied his clay, becoming their manager. The pottery was renamed and marked 'Essex Art Pottery', but young Bingham never made a go of it and the firm finally closed down in 1905, selling off all the stock. A younger son, who had emigrated to the United States, told his brother of the delights of the New World, so off he sailed with his wife and 16 children and so the aged originator of Hedingham ware, widowed in 1902, was left all alone in his cottage.

That eccentric man, now in his eighties, built a little oven and took to his wheel to make pots again. In the Braintree Museum there is an unglazed flower basket inscribed 'East Anglian Pottery made by E W Bingham, 1905', which proves the point. But the family prevailed upon him to join them and his letter of 27th April, 1906, sent to his old friend, the Hedingham village postmaster, is a happy account, not only of improvement in health - "... Can walk without a stick, run upstairs and all manner of brisk achievements..." - but also of the vastness and the grandeur of New York - "... I am sure many in Hedingham would never believe there could be such a place..."

If you see a piece of pottery inscribed on the bottom with the name Bingham, or a representation of Hedingham Castle, or the name 'Royal Art Pottery Works', 'The Unique Art Pottery' or 'East Anglian Pottery' buy it and run your fingers over it, appreciating that Edward Bingham would have done just that as he took it from the kiln.

The Historical Essex Jug made by Edward Bingham

Richard Sutton Cheek, born in Dunmow in 1826 or the following year, was in Witham by 1848. The young man may not have made a great splash, but in 1859 he must have caused a few ripples in setting up a printing shop in the basement of what is now 53 Newland Street. That he was already in this line of business somewhere in the town is shown by the entry in the County Directory of 1855:

"CHEEK, Richard Sutton, printer, bookseller & stationer, bookbinder & agent to the Conservative Land Society."

What he was like physically we do not know; no photograph or portrait has survived. That he was hardworking and business-like seems evident from the records existing. They tell that by 1870 Richard had removed to 70 Newland Street, where it meets Guithavon Street. He bought it, with other property in Guithavon Street, from the trustees of the late J H Pattisson in 1859. In his new premises he prospered; the 1861 Census shows that he was still a bachelor and 'printer, bookseller, stationer, binder and newsagent employing one man and two lads'. His widowed mother, Mary Cheek, lived with him as his housekeeper and was still alive, aged 74, at the next Census of 1871. For a time his sister, Eliza, 2 years his junior, helped him in the shop.

A century ago the discount store had as much attraction as it has today; Richard Cheek offered notepaper and envelopes at 'Immense Reduction in the Prices!!' - and even 'A large and varied assortment of Prayer Books and Church Services, suitable for presents, at greatly reduced prices'. His slates, usually sold for 8d., went at 5d, and his purses ranged all the way from one penny to half a guinea. Anyone ordering magazines at Cheek's to the value of sixpence or more a month received their free copy of 'Tomtit' - and it is only through **Tomtit** that Richard Sutton Cheek survives in the memory and has a place here.

Can you think of a less likely title for a local newspaper than **The Tomtit for the Girls of the Period and Young Men of the Day**? This was the full name of the paper that Richard Cheek got out every month, price one halfpenny, not only to advertise his and other Witham shopkeepers' wares, but also to air his opinions, to crack his jokes and to indulge in a little local gossip.

The first issue has fascinating tit-bits of information. The Saints' days are explained and the significance of Easter in our calendar; for example, "Hot cross buns are probably a relic of paganism. In London they are eaten for breakfast on this day; and the superstition that a cross bun preserved from one Good Friday to another will prevent an attack of whooping-cough has some believers still." But in amongst this potpourri of useful and interesting information, there is a hint of the gossip presently to be offered; "Tomtit will be inclined to expose any humbug, committed by great or small, eminating [sic] either from mansion or from cottage." Page one of that first issue ends on a grand note: "TOMTIT will use his influence (and that he has no doubt is great) with Mr GLADSTONE, so that he will reduce taxes... Will also confer with Mr DISRAELI, that when he again becomes HER MAJESTY'S chief adviser, it is hoped he will as usual, get us out of all the troubles into which his predecessors may have plunged us, and promote in our midst, both PEACE and PLENTY."

By the next issue in April, 1869, increased in price to one penny, the Cheekiness had increased. Illegitimate births were recorded with 'Basket' printed after them in brackets. The Witham Rifle Corps comes in for a lot of punning reference to the re-formation of its band. A tongue-in-cheek sentence at the foot of the page implies royal patronage: "We learn from good authority TOMTIT has found his way to OSBORN HOUSE." He even reports on Victorian graffiti, saying that a tombstone solemnly inscribed:

"Remember man, that passeth by
As thou is now, so once was I;
And as I is, so thou must be,
Prepare thyself to follow me"

had been desecrated by some vandal with the addition:

"To follow you's not my intent,
Unless I know which way you went."

The 3rd edition, in May, claimed a circulation of 2,000, all around Witham and Braintree district. In September a typical veiled allusion to local scandal appears: "NOTICE. To be exhibited nightly, between the hours of 8 & 10 p.m., opposite the King's Head Hotel, Maldon, A <u>Cross</u> man. Parents who have forward daughters - Husbands who have inconstant wives, and swains engaged to lady flirts are requested to keep a sharp look out! Respectable ladies are advised to pass by on the other side."

In November this little piece was published:

"MALDON. Petty Sessions - Sept. 29. Robert Smith, jun. [the Mayor's son] pleaded guilty to trespassing on lands belonging to Mrs Pattinson, in pursuit of game... We wonder what little <u>game</u> he could be after there on a Sunday morning... Could it be two-legged, or, might it be four-legged game he was in search after?" On the same page a simulated 'advertisement' refers to the same 'Bob' in the form of a stallion available at stud! Naturally enough, great exception was taken to these sly remarks and Cheek found himself summoned, with just one day's notice, to appear at Witham Petty Sessions to answer the charge of 'publishing a false and defamatory libel on and upon Robert Smith, the younger, currier, of Maldon'. The prosecutor, addressing the bench, said how unfortunate it was that "... the wife of a most respectable tradesman in Maldon has been mixed up in this matter..."

The Bench heard all the evidence, including the explanation of the printing in code of supposed letters to and from the Mayor's son and the tradesman's lady which the editor of the **Essex Chronicle**, reporting the case, thought too disagreeable for him to print, though today we find them harmless enough. The code was easy to crack; a translation would run, 'My dear Bob, I am so dull without you. Will you come this evening at seven? It does not matter if my old man is at home. I shall have a fire and a nice spring-bottom'd sofa ready in the best room... my children will in bed and we can enjoy ourselves I hope to our hearts' content.' Bob's reply was, 'My dear Mrs War--n, You really must excuse me as I have had so much of it lately my doctor advises me to rest awhile. I will come tomorrow evening the 14th about seven if my doctor can brace me up for the occasion...' The outcome was that Richard Cheek was remanded on bail to the next assizes.

Yet Tomtit continued unconcerned, though December's issue gives a clue that something is in the wind, with a leader in large print on public opinion and the necessity for it to be respected in spite of its waywardness: "**Tomtit** has, in less than 10 months, without either 'pushing it', or by advertising it in the least degree, attained a wide circulation. It is therefore with some reluctance that we feel disposed to separate ourselves from so large a connection; but we are reminded of the fact that whenever our acts endanger the quiet and safety of others, it is worse than selfishness on our part, to continue a course which might involve them in any degree of trouble or inconvenience." The cheeky bird chirped cheerfully and independently into 1870. When the town of Chelmsford bought itself a new fire engine, Tomtit twitted: "What they do when they have an extensive fire. They get out the engine -

attach four horses - prepare themselves with postillions - light their lamps - and cry:-'Where are the brigade?'..."

In February, 1870, **Tomtit** had the nerve to publish a poem on the 'Evils of Gossip':

She who stands lounging at the door,
And gossips precious time away,
Perhaps is laying up a store
Of sorrow for another day...

and while Cheek himself was awaiting his trial for spreading libellous gossip! The case came up at the Assize in March, 1870; he changed his plea to guilty and got off very lightly, having to undertake to sell no more copies of the offending issues of September, October and November and to enter into a recognizance of £100 to this effect.

So, suitably chastened, the journal continued to entertain its readers with heavy jokes and punning comments. In May, 1870, for example, the gallimaufry offered included a hint for the prevention of gnat bites, a soulful poem entitled 'Up in the Attic' and riddles like these:

"Q: Why is the letter D like a sailor?

A: Because it follows the C.

Q: Why should railway travellers invariably avoid the 12.50 train?

A: Because it is ten to one if they catch it."

There is also a long and serious article on 'Our apology for satire' in which, somewhat ruefully, Cheek says, 'The essence of law is altercation; for the law can altercate, fulminate, deprecate, irritate and go on at any rate.' This is the nearest that Richard Cheek gets to any mention of his brush with the law, and this may have been Tomtit's farewell speech, for this is the last issue to be published as far as can now be established. No doubt his old mother was glad that he stopped bringing such notoriety to the business and the family.

When Richard actually gave up the business altogether is not exactly known. It seems that by 1881 John Day was occupying his shop, although he was still the owner. It may be that illness forced him into retirement, for he died on 8th May, 1893, in his 66th or 67th year. His printing and stationery business was then bought by Bernard Clark Afford and his shop is remembered with affection still, as Witham's principle place for cheerful chat and glorious gossip.

Colony House

Purleigh lies just ten miles southeast of the county town, where it has existed unobtrusively for more than a thousand years. Yet this place connects England, America and Russia in an interesting way and that not so very far back in its story. So let us not dwell upon its ancient history, simply noting in passing that it gets its name from those first Saxon settlers who found its forest abounded in 'pur' - birds of the snipe family.

Through the centuries the church, founded and built by Saxons when they took the Christian faith in the 7th Century, has been repaired and rebuilt as faith dictated and finance permitted. In its old records, of which one precious fragment records burials in the high and breezy churchyard as far back as 1592, the cavalcade of village history marches before our eyes as we turn the parchment pages. The hopefulness of baptisms, the happiness of marriages and the dismay of death are here, to sketch the rise and fall of families who have called Purleigh 'home' for hundreds of years.

In 1892 that church of All Saints, described by the county directory as 'a fine example of 13th century Decorated style', replacing Saxon and Norman buildings, with its 15th Century pillars in the chancel and an interesting Elizabethan brick porch, was fully restored once again, and that is how Purleigh's American connection was pleasantly pointed up. The money for the repair of the 'ambitious embattled west tower', as Nikolaus Pevsner called it, was raised by Americans in thankful memory of the fact that Lawrence Washington, the great-grandfather of their first President, was rector here from 1632 until 1643, when the Parliamentarians threw him out of the living. Small wonder that his son emigrated to the New World where men could freely practice their religious beliefs.

Just after that demonstration of American interest in Purleigh, the Russians invaded. Not in hordes of screaming soldiers, but in a small group of rather self-effacing, inoffensive people, including a number of English friends and sympathisers, who were looking for a quiet place where they could be at peace with the local population and practice their philosophy of self-sufficiency.

The movement started in Croydon, where a group of people were meeting regularly, English and Russian, headed by William Sinclair and John Kenworthy, men who wished to turn from the selfishness and insincerity of the capitalist, acquisitive society then all too apparent in London and its suburbs. Apparently it was Kenworthy's original idea to form a colony and put their theories of life together to the test. Having drawn together enough people interested in taking the big step of throwing in their lot as one, he framed a constitution for such a colony, circumscribed in fourteen carefully worded points of which two will suffice to set the scene:

"The Brotherhood. Constitution of the Purleigh Colony.

1. The objects are to form a colony to carry on agriculture and other pursuits as far as possible on communal grounds...

7. Any private personal property of any colonist remains his, but if he desires any articles or things which he allows to be used by other colonists, or to be mixed with colony property to remain his own, he must lodge a schedule and declaration to that effect with the secretary otherwise he will be considered to have given them to the colony."

Now all they had to do was to make for Purleigh, where they could withdraw from the world. In those days the area was remote enough for such a withdrawal, especially on the fringes of the parish away from the village itself. It was purely an agricultural area, running into depression and neglect as food prices dropped, so land was going cheap. The importance of former crops like coriander, caraway and teasel, the latter essential to the once-powerful Essex cloth trade, had long passed into oblivion. The influence of one man already living in Essex may have pointed the colonists in this direction. He was Aylmer Maude, traveller in Russia, translator of Tolstoy and a great friend of Russian exiles in Britain. He had built a house in the Russian style at Great Baddow, in which a distinguished group of Fabians often met. He had been praised by the brother of one of the colonists: "Aylmer Maude was indeed a great benefactor to the Colony. He began by inviting the colonists to dine daily at his table, and this led later on to the erection of an open-air kitchen on the Colony land, where Mrs Maude, assisted by one of the men, daily cooked the dinner..."

So it was that, in 1897, the group bought some 16 acres of land in the parish of Purleigh from a Mr Nunn, of which 10 acres lay on one side of the road from Cock Clarks to Cold Norton and 6 acres on the other. Cock Clarks is a hamlet, a cluster of cottages 2 miles west of Purleigh village. The derivation of its name goes back to two local landowners in the 14th Century, John Coke and John le Clerk. How surprised they would have been if they could have seen the hopeful little crowd of Russians go into their fields and set up their tents and their field-kitchen. At first the members of the group, the pathfinders so to speak, were unattached men only. They rented what local cottages they could and occupied them in small groups. One contemporary account explains, "The young men lived in the hamlet of Cock Clarks, half a mile from the Colony land. They lived a life of Spartan simplicity, 5 shillings per week being the maximum a man was supposed to spend on his keep."

Quickly they broke their land and sowed their seed, including kitchen vegetables as well as cereals; then they began to build their first house, still existing as Grey House. Colony House, as it is called today, stands on the other side of the road, another solid reminder of the skill of these young Russian settlers. Within a year the first family unit of the Tolstoyan community was installed in that first house and the pioneers went on to build a large 'carpentering shop' and a poultry house, the former designed by J C Kenworthy himself. The determination of these young men to make a success of their colony in a life of self-sufficiency is shown by their discovery of brickearth in one of their fields. From that place they dug the clay to make the very bricks of that first house. Farmer Nunn put the situation in a nutshell, "You would have been amused to see those chaps treading the pug there with their bare feet - men of refinement and education; some of them with high social positions and good income, which they have given up for this kind of life."

The first family came from the original Croydon Brotherhood, William Hone with his wife and four children. As other houses were built the Anglo-Russian colony grew to a satisfying total of 88 people. At this time one of the houses, Hill Farm, was extended, as can still be seen today, to house the printing press needed to produce their periodical **The New Order.** They also printed some of Aylmer Maude's translations of Tolstoy, the profit from which went to furthering the aims of the colony. It is revealing to learn that with all those acres to be ploughed and hoed, the only extra power the men could call upon was one horse, named Johnny. He was so used to pulling a London bus in his youth that they had the greatest difficulty in breaking him of the habit of pulling a plough at the same speed.

Though the idea of exiled Russian princes

hewing wood and drawing water brought the sightseers to the wilds of Essex, the colonists were quietly accepted by the villagers who were ready to lend a helping hand. The interest in the county was so great, however, that a young reporter on the - **Essex Chronicle** cycled over to interview the colonists and report the facts under the headline: "Another world in Essex", saying, "Although the fierceness of present-day competition and the many undesirable elements of 'business' have been deplored by numbers, not many have had the courage to openly and actively show their disapproval by declining to participate in such a system. A few there are however, who have 'dared to stand alone', and some of these have formed a little Colony at Purleigh." In an interview with Mr Aylmer Maude the reporter was told "... as the movement was still in an early phase of its existence one did not know exactly what line it would take... the Brotherhood were not Socialists, because they did not approve of a directing Governmental force, neither were they Communists, but peaceful Anarchists, taking for their guidance the Sermon on the Mount and striving to set an example of usefulness and gentleness."

Though they tried hard to develop on free, co-operative lines, it was this vagueness of intention that probably led to dissention and division - some members thought the printing of Tolstoy translations was an act of commercialism, even though they were the people who profited; others considered that the <u>selection</u> of new members went against the basic principle of their life together. A third reason for dissent was the problem of the Doukhobors, Russian refugees whom the Brotherhood was trying to help. Some of them had joined the Purleigh Colony, but when the time came for the resettlement of their sect in Canada, they went off with the main body to give them the benefit of their experience here in Purleigh.

So, diminished and disillusioned, the Colony was disbanded and, in 1899, Aylmer Maude sorrowfully wrote to Tolstoy to tell him of the failure.

Few people today could tell you of the origin of those strong-looking houses still standing along

Hackmans Road, but they are there to inspire with the ideal of those Colonists. They thought out their attitude, they formed a plan, they worked so very hard to achieve their aims - what a pity it is that human beings find it so difficult to live in harmony - in Colonies, countries or even continents!

Take a trip to Tolleshunt Darcy. Savour the peace of the place. No wonder people are reluctant to move away. Look at the local G.P.; the doctor who from his house in Tolleshunt Darcy travelled many miles over a wide area of rural Essex to bring healing and hope to countless families, rich and poor. He so loved the place and the people that he stayed and practiced his profession for close on 70 years and lived until 1932 to become a modern folk-hero in that part of Essex stretching from Totham and Tiptree to the banks of the Blackwater.

John Henry Salter was born in Arundel in 1841, of well-to-do parents. By the time he was 20 it was clear that he had before him a great career in medicine. Then he severely damaged an eye in a mysterious incident at the Derby, which has never been fully explained, though he did 'enjoy' a couple of fights with gypsies there. However, it meant that he had to have a glass eye and so the only position in medicine that he could now hope for was that of a general practitioner. So the country's loss of a surgeon was the county's gain of a family doctor: for he chose Tolleshunt Darcy as his first and, as it turned out, his last practice. He had kept a diary since he was 8 years old, so it is not surprising to see the 23-year-old, newly-qualified doctor writing: '1864. 5th July. A practice down in Essex sounds exceedingly well.'

After that, things happened in whirlwind fashion. He went on rounds with the old doctor, bought the practice from him, was initiated into Freemasonry to the second degree, bought a wedding ring and, in October, married his childhood sweetheart, Laura Mary Duke. How pleased he was to record on the following 29th October: 'Reached Tolleshunt Darcy, and sat down to dinner in the most cosy dining room in the world. Received with great cheering at the entrance to the village.' Within 2 days he had delivered his first baby in the village and life took on a pattern which the very young doctor could not have guessed would repeat itself for more than 60 years.

As a country doctor, he had many social obligations that he performed to the full. Even the very next month he records: 'Penny readings at Tollesbury in evening - the most dreadful ordeal we had any of us ever undergone in our lives...' But in January, 1865, he had a more cheerful report: 'Went to Barn hall to an evening party - the regular country farmer's hospitality... a tolerably successful evening. Our health given at supper. My wife looked very nice, and was a good deal admired...' Though such entertainment contrasted strongly with the sophisticated London night life enjoyed by a man of his class and upbringing, Dr Salter was always pleased to get back to the peace and friendliness and the daily urgency of his country practice. There his progress after five years was noted to this effect: 'A grand day of surgery for Essex - several important operations at home.' The patients were all continuing well a month later.

On visits to the capital and anywhere in Essex where sport was promoted, John Salter followed boxing, rowing, horse-riding and -racing, shooting, hare-coursing, dog racing and showing, fencing, football; the list is endless. He was a great, enthusiastic and able amateur sportsman. Accounts of his part in boxing or perhaps they should be called 'encounters' in public arenas, clubs, pubs and the like, are recounted with real relish. Even with one eye irretrievably put out of action he still notes 'claret' being drawn and eye being blacked while he gave a good account of himself. As to his following of luckless horses, one dreadful day at Goodwood goes into his diary with the comment, '... the conclusion I came to was that horse-racing as regards backing horses is altogether a mistake.'

He surrounded himself with dogs and cats from the outset and took an active part in all the pursuits of a country gentleman. So he shot all round the county and took his hounds to coursing contests, at which he was consistently successful. He was a man of such tremendous energy that he could indulge in all these interests, at the same time carrying out all his obligations to his patients. It was in October, 1872, that, whilst driving his trap through Kelvedon, he came up with '... crowds of people carrying off wounded men and women from the railway accident which had taken place one hour before...' He spent 7 hours at the scene, a professional presence of the utmost value.

His diary reflects an innocent wonder in the world and its ways. A good example is the entry: '1873. November 18th. In the evening I went into Chelmsford to see 'A living skeleton' who was being exhibited at a twopenny show... He was certainly the most extraordinary mortal I ever saw - 32 years of age, 49 lbs in weight, and his head, arms and legs complete skeletons... It was such an extraordinary case that I sent him to the College of Surgeons and other scientific places in London, and he got a considerable income by going to various societies and being examined...' People's faith in him as a doctor was justified time and time again. On one occasion he dashed down to Goldhanger, where a boat had capsized and a man was brought ashore quite unconscious. For four hours he gave that man artificial respiration and so restored him to life and his family.

By this time he was well-known in widely differing spheres. The **Lancet** was mentioning him as an authority on diptheria at the same time as the King of Sweden was writing to him to order some of his famous dogs. On 16th January, 1887, Dr Salter recorded that he was appointed to the committee of the International Sportsmen's Exhibition Dog Show 'to be held at a new hall in Kensington called Olympia'. It was there, later in the year, that he won 14 prizes with the 9 dogs he exhibited and four days later a cryptic note in the diary shows that he delivered 9 children in the space of 48 hours. He still found time to to sit on the Witham bench as a Justice of the Peace. When he was 49 he notes that he was up at six to do some gardening, a similar entry was made when he was in his eighties.

A further entry helps us round out his character. "1895. Sept. 12th. Coming back from a confinement at midnight came across a chap lying in the road, dead beat - a tramp just out of prison. I scandalised my man by making him take the poor chap up and bring him home, walking myself, and then giving him a 'blow out' of grub and a shilling! Wrong or right it gave me pleasure to do it, and did the poor old chap no harm." That same day he was having the new-fangled telephone put in. He was ever young in mind when it came to trying new inventions. In 1896, in his fifties, he had his first ride on a tricycle, 'round the lawn 20 or 30 times at quick speed without any assistance' and in the following January 'saw the moving photographs at the Alhambra, which are wonderful'.

In January, 1898, he made the first of many trips overland to Russia, invited by the Muscovites to judge at one of their great dog shows. He was welcomed by the Grand Duke Nicholas and taken shooting there. The wolves and a bear he bagged were stuffed for him and sent home. That unfortunate bear can still be seen in the Chelmsford & Essex Museum; one of the few surviving relics of the Salter collection which was formally opened by Prince George at the Museum in 1932.

So the story of his busy life runs on. "1902. Jan 15th. Up at 4 a.m., and wrote my contribution to the **Essex Victoria History** on 'Wild fowling'... July 28th... went to London to look at a motor - a Benz Ideal, $4\frac{1}{2}$ horse power... with a driver to take us out of the traffic of London, started for home... cost me £239.5s.' And in August, 'I shall not rest until I get the Salcot people a good supply of water.'

With a loving wife supporting him, Dr Salter took life by the scruff of the neck and fairly wrestled from it happiness, excitement, fantastic friendship and a lot of fun. But there is a very sad entry in his diary when he recorded the illness and death of his beloved partner: 'Oct. 3rd. The funeral - the most sorrowful day of my life. Every affection and respect paid to her, as she deserved.' As he wrote he could never have guessed that his life as a widower would last for another 30 years. He took each one as it came, making the best of it, administering to hundreds of grateful country folk in an area widespreading round Tolleshunt Darcy.

On his 80th birthday, the whole village assembled to pay tribute to him, expressing their feelings for him in the shape of a silver lamp. He was much loved and took an innocent delight in writing, '... found the **Essex Chronicle** had a portrait and a little sketch of me in it, calling me 'the G.O.M. of D'Arcy...' which he truly was, and which he continued to be until his ninetieth birthday and beyond. Then on the 13th of the following April he passed peacefully to rest and was buried beside his wife, against the hedge running around the new burying ground across the road from the old church yard.

Dr John Salter's house in Tolleshunt Darcy

*Isaac Mead - Frances Maynard
- Evelyn Wood - Frank Crittall -
Thomas Smith - Jimmy Mason
- Laurence Oates - Thomas Clarkson -
Dorothy L Sayers - Vic Gunn*

If you are ever round the Rodings way, take the time to drive into a little bit of history . Turn off the B184 on to the lane signposted to Beauchamp Roding, drive through that village and in half a mile look for the driveway to Hornets Farm, marked on the Ordnance Survey 1:50,000 map. In the overgrown, bramble-covered corner between the lane and the drive you will discover the tombs of a farmer and his family. There in peace they lie, far away from any churchyard. Before the inscription on the one substantial stone marking the grave of Mrs Mead becomes indecipherable let the facts be recorded.

Isaac Mead was an independent small farmer in the best British tradition. He came up the hard way, working as a humble labourer for years, and scrimping and saving until he could attract a loan large enough to risk on a small place of his own. It was the desire to be his own master that drove him on, the aim to make his life wholly dependent on his own efforts. He climbed the hill of enterprise and found the view well worthwhile. In older age he had a corner of one of his fields specially consecrated, so that he and his family might find their eternal rest in the very soil that had succoured them through a successful farming life. That gesture alone gives colour to the man's character.

The Rev. Edward Gepp, writing a foreword to Mead's book in 1923, summed up: "Mr Mead is a successful man. Risen from the lowest grade of farm labourer, he has, by strenuous and intelligent exertion, become farmer, master miller, and owner of land. To whatever his success is due... there is no doubt that there were three contributory things, viz. good parents, the fear of God, and a taste for literature. A cottage boy feeding his mind on Bunyan, Defoe, Dickens and the Bible may not be so rare a thing as we generally suppose; but rare it is, and precious."

Isaac was born on 23rd January, 1859, at the Building Yard, High Easter. His earliest memory was of the wedding of the Prince of Wales in 1863, for the village entered wholeheartedly into celebration, with a procession all down the street and a special tea in the barn specially decorated with Chinese lanterns. A recollection of his later childhood was Sunday singing in the chapel: '...as very few of the old people at this time were able to read, the Clerk used to give out the number of the hymn; then he would read two or more verses out; then repeat the number; and off we started. In many cases he would read two lines out of a four-lined verse; then the singing stopped, time he read the other two lines. This was done so the poor old folk could join in the singing.' Isaac tells that his father led the singing, so there was not much doubt that Isaac made his proper contribution.

High Easter was a real village in those days, with at least 5 bootmakers, a harness-maker, a butcher, two blacksmiths, two grocers, a tailor and a draper. In his lifetime Isaac could reckon 40 small farms which were pulled down as the land was concentrated in bigger units: 'What a contrast to see the village, as then was the case, beaming with happy, contented people, young and old... always willing to do a kind act, without fee or reward.' There must be older folk in the Easters who still remember the Beards, the Sawens, and the Hockleys who grew up with Isaac Mead and his siblings.

A 9 year old could hardly appreciate the relative degrees of poverty, but when Isaac overheard his parents trying to make a choice between paying his father's 'Sick club' money or buying their boys the boots they so badly needed, he ran across to the bailiff at Bury Farm and arranged with him to start work the very next Monday. But you cannot do that sort of thing without your parents knowing straight away: they were proud of young Isaac, but assured him that they would manage somehow, while he continued his education. Before he was 11, however, he had got a job looking after sheep, weeding and cutting up thistles, all for 1s.6d. [$7\frac{1}{2}$ pence] per week. He brought that up to half a crown [$12\frac{1}{2}$ pence] a week by rising at dawn and milking all the cows six days out of seven.

Yet all that work did not make Isaac a dull boy. He skylarked about as much as any other village lad - and one day paid a dreadful price for it. He had climbed way up into an oak tree one autumn morning to help shake out the acorns for the family pig. Excited, he lost his grip and fell 25 feet to the ground. He was picked up and carried home with a broken thigh. The country doctor was a devoted man and did all he could for the poor boy. With his leg in an all-enveloping splint, and in pain that can only be imagined in our days of helpful drugs, Isaac had to find some way of making two months pass by without fretting or dying of boredom. Luckily, there was in the house a copy of Bunyan's **Pilgrim's Progress.** Not only was it an exciting read for an imaginative boy, it was also a source of great inspiration in his fight against pain and inactivity. Came the day, at last, when the splint could be removed and Isaac sat outside his door, enjoying that newfound freedom. But he was still so weak he fainted away, fell from the chair and broke that thigh again. He was learning Bunyan's message the hard way, for the splints this time stretched from his armpits to way past his foot and he was reduced to blowing soap bubbles to keep boredom at bay. He survived, the splints were removed, then he passed a month wrapped in brown paper and plaster of paris before spending another month hobbling about on crutches.

So, at last, and still aged but 13 years, Isaac was ready to go to work again, on Heron's farm. Then he and his father found jobs on Green's Farm, where Isaac now took on man's work and was paid 7 shillings a week. He soon became competent at hedging and ditching and, in 1874, had his first swing of a scythe. He wrote of it, "This is fine exercise for a young man, but hard work." Isaac proved he was tough enough to survive this testing time. It was a difficult period for the 16-year-old lad because he was working under a foreman or bailiff who thought he would break the boy's spirit by overloading him with work. He put the lad in a barn full of barley, gave him a flail and told him to thresh it out on piece rates; half a crown for every quarter threshed out. Isaac was equal to it. He set himself to work so systematically that, at the end of the week, he had earned enough to be paid in golden sovereigns — a wonderful experience for a humble, young farmer labourer.

Within a year he had moved on to a job in a windmill, where he learned the mysterious art of the miller, including the dressing of stones. The following year he proved his worth to his master by closing down the mill when a great gale suddenly sprang up. He was able to look across to White Roding and see that mill lose a sail and topple over. That job ended when the mill was sold in 1880 and Isaac moved to the Chelmsford area as he went from mill to mill seeking work. He found a place at last with the well-known firm of Marriage's, where he had to operate the windmill at Blasford Hill, Great Waltham, and the watermill, Croxton's, down below it on the Chelmer. His value was appreciated and he was made working foreman at the Springfield Mill.

Now love entered his life. Isaac found a mate back in his home village and the were soon talking of marriage and of a great desire to find their own farm, small as it might be, and to be able to-control, in a limited way, their own destiny. The chance came with the advertisement for renting of Waples Mill Farm, lying on the banks of the river at

Beauchamp Roding, now merged in a bigger holding. Isaac had been saving hard and he borrowed £200 to make up the valuation of the previous tenant's stock. He was a farmer! Now he could get married to his Susan Jane Smith. On Monday, 29th October, 1882, they walked out as one from High Easter Chapel and into Waples Mill Farm. It needed a great deal of hard work to bring it together and to scratch a living from its produce. They had miserable setbacks, like the day when a flood carried off half their hay crop, and they took on extra commitments in the shape of four sons!

Isaac's knowledge of milling came in useful when the farm did not pay, for it also had an ancient windmill and a watermill which were put to profitable work. Still there were problems. One day the floor of the watermill gave way and one harvest of barley was simply washed away. In May, 1910, the windmill was burned down through the carelessness of a steam engine driver. The farm was a family struggle to which the growing boys contributed their strength; and slowly the Mead family won the day. They were able to extend their little empire by renting Hornets Farm. Isaac says of it: "The farm, Hornets, which I last took, was in a very dilapidated state... during the past nine years I have put in the greater part of my spare time to bring this to a more creditable condition..." This was written in 1922, as part of Isaac's autobiography, **The Life Story of an Essex Lad**, which he put together when he was confined to the house after a serious accident. It gives a good picture of farming life over a period of great agricultural depression and it provokes admiration of a man who could achieve so much by sheer hard work.

He found time to help his fellow men in the work of the Parish Council when it came into being under the 1893 Act and in the achievement of allotments for villagers. He once had the honour of putting to Sir Winston Churchil personally his views on the rating or exemption of agricultural property. Those tombstones are the only monument to all that struggle, yet not quite, for in the Local History Collection of Chelmsford Library as well as a copy of that little book, there is also Isaac's own scrapbook and, in his own hand, a continuation, never published, of the Essex Lad's story. A summary of his outlook on life is found in his own words, "My sympathies have always been with men of all classes who try to leave the world better than they found it."

Little Easton lies north-west of Dunmow. It seems an insignificant little village today, but the strange fact that a few years ago the vicar had to rebury the bones of people long since dead and gone gives a clue to the place's importance in mediaeval times. Modern houses were to be built on ground which neither developers nor villagers realised was the cemetery of those canons and priors and humble monks who made up the community of the Priory founded in 1104. They are remembered today only by the south aisle of their large chapel, for it has survived to serve as the complete church for the present parish.

Once a year at least, the monks made life in Little Dunmow bustling and boisterous by holding their now world-famous and recently-revived Flitch ceremony at which married couples could compete for a great joint of bacon awarded to that couple who could most conclusively prove that they had lived in perfect harmony for the space of the last year and a day. For 364 days of the year, it seems, life in Little Dunmow flowed quietly on in rural rectitude through hundreds of years. Then along came a beautiful young lady to set the village on its ear with rumour and gossip and scandal-mongering, and to provide fun and games for those in the high social circle in which she moved.

Frances Evelyn Maynard, born in 1861, was the grand-daughter and heiress of the third and last Viscount Maynard, whose son, Henry, died in 1865, just a few months before his own demise. Time out of mind this had been the family living in the Big House, Easton Lodge, and lording it over the local peasantry. The house itself had been practically rebuilt after a disastrous fire on 31st January, 1847, and was still quite new when young Frances was roaming the park surrounding it. The park covered

12,000 acres, the drive from the road was 2 miles long, and the visitor had to run the gauntlet of herds of deer. Even the parish church stood within the park's boundary.

David Coller, writing in 1861, described the church as 'a neat and ancient building'; saying that it '... has on the south side the Bourchiers' or Bowsers' chapel, where rest some of that ancient family; but it is now used as the burial place of the Maynards, and its monuments furnish a history of the race.' He gives a full description of all those impressive monuments, but there is one there today which he could not describe, since it celebrates the subject of our story.

Valerie Flatley, writing in the **Evening Echo** in 1973, describes it as '... a marble bust that stares sightlessly towards the altar.' The inscription runs: 'Frances Evelyn Maynard, Countess of Warwick, Lady of the Manor of Estaines. Born December 10, 1861. Died July 26, 1938.' Miss Flatley adds: 'Mistress of the future Edward VII, attempted blackmailer of George V, heroine of an Elinor Glyn novel and, perhaps strangest of all, committed socialist.'

Frances said of herself in typically disarming manner, "I am descended on one side from Nell Gwynn; on the other from Oliver Cromwell. The Nell in me is all discretion. The Noll (i.e. Oliver) would fain be heard." Certainly in life she showed Nell far more often than she listened to Noll. It could almost be said that it was to her disadvantage that she grew from a leggy little girl into a strikingly beautiful young woman; and a young woman without a father's guiding hand, for he died when she was but 3 years old, and she immediately became an extremely rich heiress who knew, as she grew up, that she could marry just about anybody she pleased.

When she was 17 she was invited to stay at Buckingham Palace as a guest of Queen Victoria who was anxious to see her youngest son, Leopold, Duke of Albany, suitably married. Frances qualified both in beauty and in social standing, but, unbeknown to his Queen and mother, Leopold already had his eye on a princess. However, he did call on Frances to fulfill his duty to Mama and he took with him a handsome equerry, Lord Brooke, otherwise Francis Greville, 5th Earl of Warwick, who had just come into his majority. The lovely debutante fell for him and, in 1881, aged 20, she walked with him out of the church where Edward VII, then Prince of Wales, signed the register as a witness, and into a glittering reception numbering other royal guests among its noble ranks.

Looking back, Prince Edward's signature could be considered ominous, for 7 years later Frances was to become the mistress of the 47-year-old Prince. In those years Frances certainly hit the high spots in a veritable whirlwind of social gaiety. She moved in a high, young and daring Society, with a permissiveness which only operated in the seclusion of big town and country houses when the servants were safely tucked up in bed. "It doesn't matter what you do in the bedroom as long as you don't do it in the street and frighten the horses", was the acute observation by Mrs Patrick Campbell, celebrated actress of the period.

Following this code of behaviour, Frances had a big 'affair' with a 'well-known lord', as they would say in the gossip columns, and, when his wife came into possession of a compromising letter, Frances was able, through her connections, to ask the Prince of Wales to help her in effecting its return. The outcome of the matter was that it was patched up with 'honour' satisfied on both sides. Years later Frances wrote of that difficult meeting with the Prince, 'He was more than kind... suddenly I saw him looking at me in a way all women understand. I knew I had won, so I asked him to tea.' It was not long before the meeting had developed into another affair and, in correspondence, Frances, known by the royal lover as Daisy, was being called 'my own lovely little Daisy wife' by her infatuated protector.

They were seen together everywhere. In London, in Paris, and, of course, at Easton Lodge. Lord Brooke must have known of the liaison and was probably only reluctantly tolerant, under threat of royal disfavour, but Edward's wife, Alexandra, acknowledged the seriousness of the infatuation by studiously ignoring Frances when issuing invitations to any of her social events. The love affair appears to have been genuine while it lasted, for many letters were exchanged and they were couched in the most endearing terms, signed by the Prince, for example, as 'For ever yours, your only love.' And through it, strangely enough, Little Easton obtained the status and convenience of its own railway station.

With royal influence behind her, Frances put pressure on the railway company to provide a platform and to stop the train that regularly brought her darling Prince. She awaited him at the station in a wagonette to drive him herself up the long drive to the privacy and the gaiety where, as she says in her book **Life's Ebb and Flow**, he '...thankfully threw aside the heavy trappings of his state to revel in the love of nature.' The most marvellous scenes of pomp and splendour were witnessed by the army of servants retained to serve the Prince and his retinue. Entertainment was on a scale so vast that a few nights with well over a hundred guests to dinner, with dancing and other delights at the old family home of Warwick Castle, as well as the more modest weekends at Easton Lodge, made quite a hole in Brooke's savings.

A minor example of the reckless spending that made the Lodge one of the most sought-after weekend invitations of the 1890s was the game of chess put on for guests one sunny afternoon. The game was played outdoors, with living pieces, actors and actresses specially brought up from London and attired in sumptuous costumes for this one whim. Like so many good things, it had to come to an end. Edward was at the mercy of all the stunning, young ladies of Society, though well into his fifties by 1898. When he met Alice Keppel, a court beauty eight years younger than Frances, it seems the rather cosy domesticity of their 8 year old affair lost its attraction.

Just as they had met with discretion, so they parted with tact and stayed good friends until Edward's death twelve years later. Frances had been a King of England's 'Darling Daisy', and she must have been rather proud of it, once she had recovered from the humiliation of being supplanted. Both Edward and she were able to convince Alexandra that the last years of their relationship had been quite platonic, so Frances was once again admitted to the favour of royal invitations. But this did not have quite the same meaning for Frances because, strange to say, she had in the interim become converted to the socialist way of life. Actually, she had tried to interest the Prince by taking him to talk to Joseph Arch, celebrated founder of the Agricultural Labourers' Union. This could have been a contributory cause of Edward's breaking off the liaison.

Her interest in socialism was manifested in 'good works', rather than in reducing her own standard of living to meet her growing debts. As Miss Flatley says, "She wanted for nothing in a whirl of extravagance, dressed by Worth, painted by Sargent and sculpted by Rodin." But she did have a talent for understanding the hopes and fears of ordinary working people and she did throw herself heartily into schemes to assist them. A year before the break, Frances had paid for the setting up of a secondary school at Dunmow, this at a time when less than two children in a hundred, on average, had the chance of senior school education in Essex. She endowed a home for crippled children and a school of needlework where girls could be paid for the work they produced which was sold in a shop in Bond Street, so saving them from the grim alternative of the life of a 'skivvy' in service to the very gentry she knew so well.

It was Robert Blatchford, editor of the - **Clarion**, who was instrumental in converting Frances to the cause of socialism and the improvement of life for ordinary people. His paper had carried a swingeing attack on the 'idle junketings' going on at Warwick Castle in 1895 at a time of much unemployment in particularly bitter weather. She hied off to London to give him a piece of her very determined mind, but he made her listen - for most of the day; and she later explained: "My old ideas and ideals were all brought to nought."

So she became deeply interested in politics, joining the Social Democratic Party, speaking at conferences, presenting pensions to veteran miners, campaigning for free school meals for children. At the same time, she and her husband were buying Studley Castle in Warwickshire with its 340 acres, so that it might be used as an agricultural college solely for women; a hostel was also opened in Reading for women wanting to study horticulture and agriculture. There is no doubt that, in her attitude to the liberation of women, she was very much ahead of her times. Yet, at the age of 42, she was to have a baby, sister to another daughter who was married before this new baby was born. A couple of years later she was touring the country energetically canvassing in the election, and being disappointed by the meagre number of seats they won. But she kept up the fight, even when she was over 60; in 1923 she contested a seat as a Labour Party candidate against the up-and-coming Anthony Eden. Inevitably, she lost the day.

That she was a woman of indomitable spirit is shown by the fact that, even before the Great War, she was finding it difficult to make ends meet. She had used up her fortune in years of lavish entertaining and, using her name and reputation, had run up bills totalling the colossal sum of £48,000. Yet still she maintained the standards of what she considered reasonable hospitality and of generosity to the less-privileged - so something had to be done. Frances had kept all the letters Prince Edward had written and, though he was now dead, they would have caused a sensation had they been published: and what a price they would fetch from a publisher in an advance on royalties! But it was not so much the publication that she intended, as the use of the idea that they might be so used.

One of her biggest creditors was a Member of Parliament. Frances told him that she had received an offer of £100,000 for the right to publish these letters. She knew he would immediately inform Buckingham Palace and she used the same channel to let it be known that she would give George V his father's letters intact for exactly that sum. Emissaries came and went until the advisers to His Majesty felt the time was ripe. By mid-1915 they obtained a Court Order that all these 'documents contained in a sealed envelope' should be destroyed. But Frances was lucky; her intermediary, Arthur du Cros, having performed a valuable service to his King, also helped Frances clear her debts, to the tune of £48,000, which was never repaid. He did, however, receive a baronetcy.

After her husband died in 1924 the hostess-turned-socialist lived on at Easton Lodge, open house for socialist politicians and trades union leaders. In 1935 5,000 working people went to a gala day there, standing on the very steps where once a future king had posed for the photographer in a rich and intimate circle of friends, including 'Darling Daisy'. By this time Frances was a stout dowager, living in a great house sadly in need of repair and maintenance, feeding her beloved ponies from her front door and letting her dogs sleep in a four-poster bed. Yet still she was ready to act in the socialist cause, opening fetes, shows, public buildings and so on almost up to her death in 1938 aged 77. Whatever one may think of Frances and the morals of the age and society in which she lived, it can be said with conviction that she certainly put Little Easton on the map!

The village of Widford has been bisected by the A12, developed as an industrial estate,and practically swallowed up in Chelmsford's expansion. Yet its separate identity can be seen in three places where a hint of the old village life persists: in the church on one side of the main road, in the green-painted, corrugated-iron village hall down the village street on the other side and, not far from it, in the 'Sir Evelyn Wood', an unspoiled village pub still retaining its old-fashioned furniture, its tiny rooms and its atmosphere of genuine interest and concern of the landlord and customers in each others' affairs.

The traffic on the main road dashes by ignorant of its attractions and equally uninformed about its sign, the only one in the world, and the reason for it being so named. Those travellers are the losers, for behind the name lies the story of a great man of Essex. This old beerhouse had formerly been called 'Rose Hill', until it was bought by the Gray family of brewers. They changed the name and gave the house its sign, shown for the first time in the 1881 directory of Chelmsford as the 'General Wood Inn'. Since it was in 1879, that the General was presented with a Sword of Honour by the County, it is quite likely that that event inspired the Grays to celebrate it in this happy manner, though what the tenant of the time, James Mead, thought of the idea has not been recorded.

The tenant of today, Harold Taylor, proudly keeps behind the bar a book published in 1900 entitled **Celebrities of the Army** because it includes a fine portrait of General Sir Henry Evelyn Wood, V.C., G.C.B., G.C.M.G., and an account of his life. He keeps it there because the man is his sign and symbol, so to speak, but also because Evelyn Wood is a man to be proud of, and Essex born and bred. It was in February, 1838, that John and Emma Wood had a son. In his autobiography published in 1906, Wood sketches in his boyhood:

"I was born at the Vicarage, Cressing... the youngest son of John Page Wood, Clerk in Holy Orders, who was also Rector of St Peter's, Cornhill in the City of London... my father took his degree early in 1820, and was immediately appointed Chaplain and private Secretary to Queen Caroline. In the following year he married Emma Carolina Michell... In 1846, owing to monetary troubles, our governess was sent away, and her time having been previously fully occupied with the elder children, I had but little instruction, and when I went to the Grammar School, Marlborough, in February 1847, I could only read words of one syllable."

He had a lot of spirit and settled down well in the strange new atmosphere of a boys' boarding school, but in December, 1851, a harsh and unmerited flogging so affected his sense of fairness that he begged his parents to allow him to leave school, offering, in his desperation, to 'go into a London office, Green's Merchant Service, or anywhere,' to avoid remaining under the Head Master. They reluctantly agreed and, while looking round for a position for him, received an unexpected nomination for a commission in the Navy - perhaps through the good offices of his uncle who was a serving officer. But first he had to attend a 'crammer' for arithmetic, which he had not learnt at Marlborough, prior to the naval examination. He passed it in April, 1852, and by 20th May had joined H.M.S. **Victory** and been transferred from it to H.M.S. **Queen**, a first-rater of 116 guns, 'the smartest three-decker in the Fleet.'

After two years of training and subsequent service, he sailed with the Fleet and was sent ashore in the Naval Brigade at the Crimea. It is likely that he found himself in this situation because his uncle, Captain Frederick Michell, commander of the **Queen**, disappointed that he personally could not take part in the land operation himself, was determined that the family should still be represented by this 16-year-old lad. His task was to man one of the guns firing on the Russians established 1200 yards away on the heights overlooking the Balaclavan plain. Even at that young age he showed great courage under the Russian counter-barrage, fetching ammunition, putting out a fire sparked off by an enemy shell and pressing forward in an attack upon the enemy positions.

He had a particularly unpleasant experience when trying to steady his telescope to scan the opposing forces. He rested his arm on the shoulder of one of the seamen under his command and the man's head was at that very moment blown off by a Russian shell.

The young midshipman survived the most terrible conditions in camp in the Crimea. In June, 1855, still there, and brought to such weakness by disease that he could hardly stand, he mustered his last resource of energy to take part in the unsuccessful attack on the redan. All the other officers of the Naval Brigade were killed before they had covered the first 300 yards. Young Wood was wounded in the hand when a bullet shattered his drawn sword, his only weapon, but on he ran, attaching himself to a party of bluejackets with a scaling ladder. He never managed to climb it as a $5\frac{1}{2}$ ounce bullet, practically a cannon ball, struck him on the elbow, severely injuring his arm and causing him to fall unconscious. A loyal corporal dragged him back to the lines and doctors prepared to amputate his arm. Wood entirely rejected such a proposal, despite the pain he was in as it would have meant an end to his career. After a stay in hospital, he recovered sufficiently to be moved out to his old ship under his uncle's watchful eye.

His courage had not gone unremarked. Lord Raglan sent his own carriage to take the young midshipman down to the beach for embarkation and he wrote to the boy's uncle: "I was very glad to have had the opportunity of being even the smallest degree useful to your nephew, whose distinguished career cannot fail to enlist everybody in his favour." Armed with a copy of this letter Evelyn Wood returned to England and to full health, was able to effect a transfer from the Navy to the Army as a cavalry officer in the 13th Light Dragoons. Such an appointment meant that he was soon back in the battle area, but in Turkey he fell victim to the dreaded typhoid fever; yet he recovered from it just as he had from a long succession of wounds, illnesses and accidents.

Byron Farwell says, in his **Queen Victoria's Little Wars**, that '... Wood was the most accident- and sickness-prone officer in the British army', but adds: 'His experiences in the Crimea were to be but a brilliant beginning to a long military career.' I am sure that there was not another lad of 17 who had been twice mentioned in dispatches, wore the Crimean Medal with two clasps, and had the Legion of Honour and other decorations. He had also been recommended for the new, the ultimate, honour, the Victoria Cross, although he had to wait a little longer for that.

In October, 1856, he headed for India and the Mutiny, but it was over before the ship could reach Bombay. Disappointed, Wood had to be satisfied with minor local skirmishes. That was just as well, for at the same time he ran the gamut of the medical encyclopaedia, from aural infection, which half-deafened him, to sunstroke, toothache and indigestion. Then there were the accidents in which he was involved through his own high spirits, including an unsuccessful attempt to ride a giraffe bareback and a head-on collision with a tree while on horseback.

It was a short, hot, local action in December, 1859, that brought him the Victoria Cross. One night, with 15 men and a guide, he tracked down a robber-gang of mutineers, 80 strong, which had captured three men and was holding them to ransom. The men were rescued and the gang put to flight with several casualties and the loss of their weapons. Wood came back to his billet complaining of a toothache! Now the 22-year-old Lieutenant had six medals on his dress uniform.

In matters of matrimony, however, our hero was less dashing. Whilst on leave in England in 1860 he fell in love with Pauline Southwell, but her brother, Lord Southwell, head of the family, opposed the match as he would not become a Catholic. For four years the two did not meet or correspond then, in 1867, when he was in Ireland, he wrote to her '...explaining my unsatisfactory financial position and my feelings as a soldier, and asking her whether she would consider the question of marrying me, on the distinct understanding that she would never by a word, or even a look, check my volunteering for War Service': she, brave woman, accepted.

In 1873 he accompanied Wolseley to the Gold Coast where the Ashantis were being troublesome, even though he was still hobbling on an ankle broken in the hunting field where he so often indulged in his favourite recreation. In the Zulu Wars in 1879 Evelyn Wood, now a Colonel, commanded the left flank of a three-pronged attack and was the only successful commander in that tragic affair. His efforts were rewarded with the K.C.B.

It was during the Transvaal War in 1881, after the fall of Majuba Hill, that Wood was asked to assume command of the army in Natal. He was obliged to make peace with the Boers, much against the advice of die-hard militarists like Wolseley. Queen Victoria held him in high esteem, saying, "Sir E Wood is a remarkably intelligent man; not only an admirable General with plenty of dash as well as prudence... He is most agreeable as well as amusing, very lively yet very discreet." He carried on through one campaign after another, winning admiration and honours. After being appointed supremo of the Egyptian Army from 1882, he set about its complete reorganisation on the British pattern. From 1886 onwards 'that redoubtable old warhorse', as Farwell calls him, was brought back to England and held home appointments, culminating in his appointment to Field Marshal in 1903.

He had kept up his contacts with friends and relatives in Essex and thoroughly enjoyed, in younger days, hunting in the area of Harlow and the Roding Valley. Essex connections of a more formal kind included a grand dinner in his honour, mentioned in his autobiography: "1879... On the 14th October the County of Essex entertained me at Chelmsford, presenting me with a handsome Sword of Honour and a Service of plate and, in a speech at dinner, while thanking the inhabitants of Essex, I replied to the adverse anonymous critics who had objected to me naming my comrades in previous speeches by explaining the necessity for bringing the Nation into closer contact with its private soldiers. I had long thought that with a Voluntary Army it was useless to expect the best results, unless where bravery and devotion to the interests of the country is concerned, all ranks receive consideration, and I deliberately acted upon the conviction, in spite of adverse criticism." In this attitude he was ahead of his time and popular with the army and the public.

On Saturday, 4th July, 1903, the streets of the county town were crowded with citizens waiting to welcome the old, much-decorated hero as he passed on to the Shire Hall to be met by the Mayor and Corporation and have presented to him the Freedom of the Borough 'in recognition of his distinguished services in the Army and of his promotion to the rank of Field-Marshal.' Ten years later he was back in Chelmsford to present, on behalf of the County of Essex, a set of silver drums to the Essex Regiment. He was then 75. He lived quietly through a war in which he would dearly have loved to be of service, to die shortly before his 82nd birthday, on 2nd December, 1919. A list of his honours, appointments and awards would be so long as to be tedious. Let our appreciation be put into words by an unknown Essex poet, writing a collection of verses for the Bishop of Chelmsford's Appeal Fund in 1932. The life of the great man is summed up in two verses:

"If he felt fears he showed them but to God,
Beneath whose banner openly enrolled,
Where Duty showed the path, he firmly trod.
Nor swerved for pleasure, praise, or lure of gold.

And as he rode across our Essex fields,
Choosing his line, not following the crowd -
So in his aim he held to Faith, that shields
Pure souls from shame, come glory or the shroud."

Sir Evelyn Wood

Crittall today is not so much a surname as a synonym for double-glazing, but there was a day in the 1860s when that name was nothing more than the sign above a Braintree ironmonger's shop. It was a little more than just a hardware shop even then though, for tacked on at the back was a blacksmith's shop, together with all the paraphenalia needed by a tinsmith, a hot water fitter, a gas fitter and a plumber. This diversity encompassed a staff far greater than the shopper in Braintree would appreciate; three Crittalls, eight Bloomfields, from grandfather to grandson and two apprentices whose parents had to pay £100 for the privilege.

It all began with Frank Crittall who was born at West Wickham, Kent, where his father had followed his grandfather as landlord of the Swan Inn. He was apprenticed to an ironmonger in Brentford, after which he was fortunate in that he had the wherewithal to look around for his own business. He took time to choose carefully; settling, in 1848, on the very old ironmongers at 27 Bank Street, Braintree, then being run by Mrs Shave and dating back to 1665. Though there were 10 blacksmiths, 4 whitesmiths and 4 ironmongers already in this market town, Frank found his place and prospered. He became a respected figure in the town, serving on the Local Board of Health, precursor of the town council, and acting as honorary, unpaid, secretary to the Mechanics Institute, the technical college of his day. In daily life, as in his business, he practised thrift and brought up his family strictly, religiously, and fairly.

It cannot be supposed that the birth of his eighth child and third son, Francis Henry, on 27th July, 1860, made more than the merest ripple on the waters of life in Braintree in days when such large families were unavoidable. On looking back, Frank the younger recalled just one square meal a day, at noon, supported early and late, by bread 'with butter spread as lightly as a butterfly.' Only father was ever afforded the luxury of an egg. As eighth child, Frank came in for all the hand-me-downs from father, via his elder brother, with help at odd times from a large uncle given to wearing lurid checks that sat garishly and somewhat superfluously on the youngster.

When he was 7 Frank was enrolled at College House, Braintree, on the London Road between Grenville Road and the Wheatsheaf Hotel. For six years the boy endured what he called 'the most miserable, tortured, fear-racked and altogether damnable period of my life.' The only improvement engendered by the experience was his handwriting which developed to a standard of real beauty. At 13 the transfer from that day school to a boarding school at Chipping Hall, Witham, was, he said, 'like emerging from a dark and noisesome cavern into the sun-washed fragrance of a spring day.' He loved Mr & Mrs Blackie for their teaching with kindness and by example - beatings were but a bitter memory.

Frank reports, disarmingly, that he was a 'dull young dog, constantly bewildered by the several forces seemingly ranged against him - parents, school master, fellow scholars, brothers and sisters and the taboo code of Braintree nonconformity'. It makes the man all the more likeable, as does his remark 'In latter years, perky young newspapermen have interviewed me with the object of discovering that the young Crittall was a positive, alert, pushful and go-ahead youth with success as his second name. Alas, they found me a poor interviewee. Nothing in my youthful character or achievement led me or anyone else to imagine that I should ever be more than a local tradesman or craftsman.' But Frank was being modest, for the one great asset he had from childhood was his retentive memory added to a very good head for figures.

Looking ahead, Frank wanted to be a builder, though his mother thought he would make a fine nonconformist minister. Such dreams were shattered because his father's failing health required Frank's presence in the business. So, on 6th June, 1876, he started at the shop, helping his brother Richard. The work was hard and menial, including such jobs as cleaning and refilling the oil lamps left by local housewives: "Oh, the memory of the gallons, the lakes, the oceans of paraffin I must have measured out in that dark and many-scented shop!" Working a regular 77-hour week Frank learned, not only the business of the shop, but also that of the mysterious department at the back where the smiths were so busy. At 7 in the morning he was there to open up the shop and at 8 at night he was still there to lock up, Saturdays included. His 'half-day' off was from 4 o'clock on Thursdays, when the shop closed early. His pay then was two shillings a week.

Yet Frank still found time for sporting interests. It was he who, with Robert Johnson, convened the meeting in 1878 that led to the formation of the Braintree Football Club of which he eventually became goalkeeper and captain. He also helped in the establishing of the Bicycle Club, winning the first race it staged with his brother Richard a close second. When Richard, who had inherited the business on their father's death, got married, Frank had to move out of the family home into rooms in Bocking. He continued to work under Richard, who was increasingly drawn to London in business deals. But Frank found the small world of ironmongery in Braintree too confining; he let Richard appoint John Newman to take over his work and went off to Birmingham to make his own way in the world. There he obtained a post with Peyton & Peyton, manufacturers of iron goods, where he managed much of the correspondence and dealt with the progress of orders, getting just the experience he was going to need.

Then he fell in love with Ellen Laura Carter, "as gay and pert as a kitten and as pretty as a pansy, she wound me round her little finger in the first hour of our meeting." They had such happy times together at theatres and concerts in Birmingham and on bicycle outings into the countryside. He was managing now, in lodgings, on 30 shillings a week, plus the pound a week produced by the interest on the one thousand pound share in the Braintree business left him by his father. After a year had passed, a letter from John Newman back in Braintree reminded him that he had promised to go into partnership with him if a suitable business came up. One had, and Frank was the kind of man to keep a promise, so very soon he found himself in Chester, while romance continued by post.

In 1883, after only a year in Chester, there came a bolt from the blue. Richard wrote to say that he was off to London permanently and that Frank could, if he wished, take up an option on the Braintree business. Of course, Frank could not resist, but on taking over he found that the firm was severely hampered by lack of capital. Luckily local grocer, Arthur Dyer, astutely saw the opportunity for a good investment and put £4,000 into the business as a sleeping partner, letting Frank do all the work; a difficult association that lasted 40 years. So, at the age of 22, and at the shortest notice, Frank Crittall took over the business and also married his Ellen.

Now he was 'the Guv'nor' he could pursue his interest in the Back Shop where the engineering work was done. Strange to relate, it was the great Essex earthquake of 1884 that brought in much repair work and kept Crittall's afloat. Frank saw that in his business specialisation would be the secret of success, and he fixed on the production of metal windows. He was influenced by the fact that his mother, struggling with a warped, wooden sash window, had injured herself. What the damp English climate demanded for easy ventilation of home and workshop was the metal window, and what Frank needed for its development was the patronage of those wealthy people who would set the fashion. Luck was with him. Through his brother's London business, he won an order for metal windows to be supplied for Sir Hugh Adair's restoration of Flixton Hall, Suffolk, by the architect Fairfax Wade. He it was who designed the window which was to become known world-wide as the '206'.

Frank writes, "To the lay reader, 206 will be meaningless; to architects, builders and carpenters, to everyone in the many branches of the window business, 206 is instantly recognisable as the type number of the casement handle which has opened the windows of the world..." Frank also acknowledges the help of Isaac Harrington who worked with him in this new development, saying that he was "... truly the Shakespeare of metal windows. He did more than any other man to make them a factory proposition." It meant the re-equipment of the Back Shop and the installation in the cellar of a vertical steam engine to work the machines required. So, with three clerks, eight workmen, and a total wages bill of £30 a week, the metal window industry was born in Braintree. From Flixton to the world at large the windows went in ever-increasing numbers. At the same time Frank and Ellen were anxiously awaiting the birth of their boy, Valentine, in 1884.

The new business prospered, but there were such headaches in finding capital to finance expansion. There were so many ups and downs, but Frank survived them and found backers to enable him to hive off the window manufacture from the old shop as Crittall Manufacturing Company, Limited. Frank had a hard fight of it to get enough money from his other two partners, brother Richard and Arthur Dyer, to find a new site for the constantly expanding business. By 1893 it was 'gasping for room', as he put it, and so Manor Works was built and leased out to the company by a Mr Parmenter, who was a Director and also a builder. It cost £3,000 and covered a third of an acre, so it was a tremendous expansion, yet by 1934 the factory had extended all around to over four times that area.

The Guv'nor, as Frank was called by all his workmen, was still doing a 12-hour day to ensure the success of the new factory and he did have to battle with his directors on their behalf. For example, he suggested that the factory should be heated for the comfort and better performance of his workers. The board was horrified, but when that heating was installed, he was proved right in business as well as in welfare, for production zoomed where in winter it had fallen away, and the place had a high reputation for concern for the well-being of its workers. It was at this time that Frank was able to buy out his brother, get control of the company, and move it in the direction and at the speed he thought best. One of the first big contracts he won was for the fitting of metal windows in the Public Record Office. Soon the National Gallery, the Admiralty and even the kitchens of the House of Commons were to proclaim the craftsmanship of the Crittall Company.

That Frank was not a cold-hearted, money-grubbing industrialist is proved by several stories recounted in his autobiography. He had a lot of fun with family and friends. His neighbour in Bank Street was the celebrated Dr John Harrison, a real practical joker. One day when election fever was at its height, Harrison of the 'blue' faction, knowing that Frank was sporting a 'yellow' rosette, lured away young

Valentine, then but 6 years old, painted him blue all over and sat him on his trap as he went electioneering. What a hue and cry went up when the boy was missed and what exasperation when he was found! Frank and his friends got their own back - in the night they painted the front of Harrison's house, doors, windows, even the doorstep, the most vivid yellow they could find.

Crittall's steady progress became a leap when they acquired the rights to manufacture in this country the expanded metal invented by the American, Sykes. Frank was also instrumental in acquiring other associated rights in window manufacture. He journeyed to the United States in 1907 to study the market there. Now his eldest son, Valentine, came into the firm and taught the Americans the technique of window manufacture under licence, with fabulous sums being received as royalties. Total trade turnover increased from £10,000 in 1909 to £100,000 in 1914 and still the standard metal window to fit millions of ordinary houses in the country had not yet been invented.

Frank's family had now grown up and he had four sons working with him. Despite the expansion of the business, he still made his twice-daily tour of every department. On the verge of world war, Frank, aged 54, was employing over 400 workers and hovering on the brink of a world-wide marketing effort spearheaded by Valentine, who was in India seeking a way to the east for Crittall windows. The outbreak of war made him return eastwards round the world and he was able to tell his father how other firms were turning over to armaments as markets shrank in the shadow of war. Frank flung himself into the new business with patriotic fervour. He got government backing for the formation of the East Anglian Munitions Committee that organised the efforts in production of a host of small firms. By charging far lower prices for the production of shells, he was able to break the stranglehold of the disgraceful Armaments Ring and its callous attitude to profiteering from the War. He also pressed for the appointment of a Director to supervise the exploitation of scrap metal and the recovery and re-use of metal from the battlefields.

It says much for Frank's powers of organisation that within two months of the cessation of hostilities every one of about 30 firms in the consortium had ceased making munitions. As far as he was concerned it was back to windows and, though he had to start from scratch, there had been valuable lessons learned during the war in mass-production techniques. Frank planned for the big building boom with the production of a standardised window frame. He also planned an 11-acre factory at Witham for making steel office furniture which was opened in 1919. Orders for windows and doors flooded in from all over the world; a new factory was built at Maldon in 1922 and the Witham factory was converted to window-making to keep up with the demand. By 1924 Frank's little empire provided work for 1,600 people in 3 Essex factories with subsidiary companies and agencies circling the globe.

The undertaking had become too vast for one man to cope with. Reluctantly, for financial reasons, Frank had to 'go public' and spoke of 'the mixed emotions with which I saw my life's work become the gossip of the Stock Exchange and the financial press.'

After 35 years of absolute control it was hard to discuss action rather than instigate it, but Frank found other channels for his talents in the amelioration of working conditions for his people. Crittall's became one of the first factories in Essex to provide a surgery and staff to deal with general health as well as accidents; then a dental clinic was introduced, and so Frank's mind moved on to the environment in which the workers lived, dreaming of a town in the country to house the ever-increasing numbers of workpeople at the expanding Braintree and Witham factories. As Frank was not a dreamer, but a man of action, he planned the development of Silver End. Sometime before 1926, Valentine advocated the transfer of the many disabled men they employed to a special factory erected there for the manufacture of small parts. Frank enlarged on the idea, buying up 220 acres of Boar's Tye Farm. He then wrote a letter to every employee explaining that a self-contained estate would be built there and all the houses could be rented by workers or bought through weekly deductions from wages. Respect for and trust in 'The Guv'nor' elicited an overwhelming response in favour of the idea. The foundation stone of the first house was laid on 17th April, 1926, and by the end of the year 50 of the disabled men had been housed and able workers were looking forward to their new houses.

Frank had a house built for himself and his wife on a site that gave a view of the developing village and moved in in February, 1927. When 250 houses had been built the Village Hall was opened, on 10th May, 1928, by the Lord Mayor of London. A communal laundry, a co-operative store, a cinema, a restaurant and a hotel were to follow. In 1930 the completed village of Silver End held a gala in honour of Frank's 70th birthday when Mr W C Bywater said, in a speech of presentation, "Your life has been a romance of industry, activity, travel and thoughtfulness. You have demonstrated to the world that a man within his own lifetime can accomplish what would appear to be almost impossible... You have brought into being a new industry and successfully marketed a product which stands alone for quality and workmanship, with the result that you have given employment to over 5,000 people..." What Mr Bywater did not know was that Frank Crittall would find a place in social history as the first employer to introduce a 5-day working week, beating Ford's of Detroit by a good six months.

Frank closed his autobiography, in 1934, with the words: "I have had a very strenuous life – I have been blessed beyond the average." Less than a year later, on 9th March, 1935, he died on a ship homeward bound from a holiday in the West Indies. Though he was succeeded as head of his great firm by his son, Valentine, who was raised to the peerage as Baron Braintree in 1948 and died in 1961, there could be no-one who could really take the place of 'The Guv'nor'.

ESSEX PRIDE

Thomas Smith was the man who made Mayland a market garden and is destined to go down in the Essex books of history simply because he was a good gardener, and because he was backed by an American millionaire. These two men can be said to have changed the face of Essex, in particular the area around Mayland, to the extent that even today local government planners have to take into account the changes they made in the landscape.

Thomas came into the Essex scene fairly late in life. Where and when he was born we know not. He was married in 1879 and for 17 years continued in business as a self-employed printer. That business having its ups and downs and Thomas's half-conscious hankering for a life of horticultural happiness had been stimulated by an article he had read in **The Clarion** some time in 1895. It told of the rewarding life led by a smallholder on just two acres of good, old Essex soil. He could not resist the idea; he persuaded his wife to see it in the same way, sold up his house and business in the Manchester area and moved straightway to Essex, where his total capital of £800 was laid out on 11 acres of land in the parish of Mayland, which he described later as 'five of red pasture and six of weedgrown and wet arable'. On this rather inhospitable patch, with his own hands, he built a home for his wife and two children and called it The Homestead.

The sunny start was quickly clouded. The bills came in, but the hens did not lay and cows and pigs were just as unobliging. Thomas had to leave his wife to milk and muck out, while he went back to Manchester to get work as a journeyman printer. It got to be like running on the spot, very tiring and with no prospect of progress. Despite the thinly-veiled hostility of the locals to the 'townie's' efforts at self-sufficiency, the Smiths did not give up. Thomas went deeper into debt, borrowing money to finance an entirely new approach; a venture into early kitchen crops and soft fruits to catch the market when the prices were at their highest. He came back to Mayland to work on the project, taking all the extra odd jobs he could find around the village to help build up his capital. Then he spent it all again, on glasshouses for tomatoes and cucumbers, lettuces and strawberries. The dream was coming true, but there was still a long way to go and that led past John Fels' door.

Joseph Fels was an American who had made his million from the manufacture and sale of soap. He had much compassion for those less fortunate than himself and the direction of his action on their behalf may be seen from his obituary published in the **Daily News** of 24th February, 1914: "He learnt his social gospel from the works of Henry George, and he used to say that he got his impetus for its application from a meeting with Mr Keir Hardie. He was profoundly convinced that the only way in which the misery of poverty could permanently be mitigated was by the unlocking of the land for the use of the people... devoting many thousands of pounds annually to propaganda work throughout the world... Another experiment was the development of the little village of Mayland, near Althorne, Essex, on an abandoned farm of some 700 acres. Mr Fels divided the farm into about 20 smallholdings, an experimental farm, a French garden, etc. and within four years... those 700 acres were supporting a community of 300 people."

One vital need in the experiment was a really good manager. Thomas Smith saw the advertisement and applied for the job. It would seem that there was a mutual admiration here. Thomas for Joseph's generosity and determination to change society for the better and Joseph for Thomas' obvious determination, his proven ability to be self-sufficient, his practical knowledge of all the problems. Thomas became the manager of this unusual co-operative. He was very pleased as it gave him a steady income and, at the same time, offered him the opportunity of studying that intensive cultivation then known as 'French gardening', the natural extension of the very glasshouse system he already had in hand.

Fels took Thomas to Paris to see the system in operation. They were much impressed and resolved to copy it. To ensure its success, they engaged a **maraicher** or French market gardener to come over with his family and settle on the co-operative. From him Thomas was quick to learn, though some of the ideas astonished him. For example, the **maraicher** demanded 1,200 tons of manure to make a two-acre hot bed! Then again, he would grow three separate batches of melon seedlings and throw away two of them, explaining that in this way he could choose those at exactly the right stage of growth for successful transplanting.

With American money, French flair and English application the enterprise prospered and Covent Garden wholesalers snapped up Mayland melons, cucumbers and other salad crops and early vegetables. They were so good and so quick on the market that they attracted prices even higher than the original French imports. Thomas was not carried away by the initial success, he turned it to his own account by writing a book about it entitled **French Gardening** by Thomas Smith, F.R.H.S., Supervisor of the Fels Small Holdings, Manager of the Fels Fruit Farm, Windmill Nurseries and French Garden, Mayland, Essex. It came out in 1909 and a very interesting book it was, because Thomas did not glorify the system. He said in the Introduction: "Few townsmen have any conception of the labour required to make a smallholding successful. Given a strong constitution the work is healthful... but it is never other than laborious..."

How pleasant it must have been to take in his hands the solid evidence in black and white of all his experience and knowledge of the craft, gained through no little tribulation. And these difficulties continued. The **maraicher** told Thomas he would have to go back to France as his wife was homesick. Thomas was sympathetic, but did not want to lose him, so he packed them off on a fortnight's holiday back home in France at his own expense. When they did not return Thomas made enquiries and found that they never went to France at all, but simply moved down to another job at Brighton where they were offered a little more money.

It was an occasion totally beyond Thomas' control that dealt the death blow to French gardening in Essex - the Great War. It not only took away men and horses, in so doing it also took away that essential stable manure. There was compensation in that the cessation of imports gave a boost to the products of the glasshouses and a further development was that, with the success of his book, Thomas was asked to lecture on horticulture and honest-to-goodness English gardening. Into his busy mind there sprang another idea - his lecture notes could be expanded into another full-length book. The only problem, after a hard day's work, was the actual writing out of all those pages; after all he had been a printer who was still so proficient that he could set type more quickly than he could write. That was when the next idea came to him; to cut out the normal step of writing a manuscript and set the book up in type straight from his thoughts. He spent £250 of hard-earned savings on the forme and the type needed to set up just four pages at a time, made plates of those pages, re-distributed the type and started again. As Thomas himself said, "I don't suppose there was ever an author who went in search of a publisher with his book already set up and with the plates all ready for the press." A publisher presented with a work by an expert in such a finished state of preparation would thank his lucky stars - Longman's did, and the book **The Profitable Culture of Vegetables, for Market Gardeners, Smallholders, and Others** came out in 1911. It was a great success, still being published in revised editions until 1953.

The co-operative, on the other hand, was beginning to fail, due in the first place simply to human weakness and aggravated later by the onset of the Great War. Some of the smallholders began 'topping up' - putting poorer quality produce under a surface of the very best. Covent Garden merchants did not like that. Trade with them fell away, so the management resorted to direct selling in the locality, buying three horse-drawn 'lorries' to deliver all around the area. That scheme was ruined by constant thieving from the lorries at night, after they had been loaded for an early morning start. Then some of the workers began stealing the fruits of the fields even as they gathered it, so they could sell it surreptitiously on the side to make a little beer money.

Joseph Fels, who had continued a real interest in this scheme, had to admit defeat and many of the smallholdings were put up for sale individually. Thomas must have felt very badly about being let down by his own countrymen, of his own class. He returned to life on the Homestead where he and his wife continued into old age, growing and marketing their own crops while the book continued to be in great demand. Yet it was not until he was 93, in 1950, that the Royal Horticultural Society recognised his great contribution by awarding him their Veitch Memorial Gold Medal. He lived on, in retirement, to the grand old age of 98.

"WILD MAN OF THE WOODS JILTED IN LOVE SEEKS BALM IN SECLUSION" That is a headline from the **Daily Mail.** It has a modern ring about it, yet it was printed in 1904, above a story that runs: "Alone in a plantation at Great Canfield, Essex, lives a 'wild man' in the prime of life.

"Thirteen years ago he loved a woman, but she jilted him, and vowing never to look on a female's face again, he plunged into the wood to live – to brood and sigh for the love he had lost.

"The people of the district speak of him in whispers as they would of a wraith; his love story is the romance of the countryside..."

This highly dramatic piece was probably sparked off by a piece of more sober reportage in the **Essex Weekly News** of 10th June, 1904, when 'The Deemster' in his column 'Between Ourselves', wrote: "Mr James Mason, the Canfield recluse, has, I am informed, decided to leave his curious hermitage, in which he has embowered himself for the last 14 years, and to seek asylum elsewhere..."

So who was this James Mason that he should become the object of national newspaper and magazine interest? Jimmy, as he was popularly known at that time, was born in 1857, son of Richard Mason, a time-serving soldier, who liked the look of the wide-spreading, pastoral and peaceful village of Great Canfield and bought the house called Sawkins at Puttocks End in 1853. That was in the days when the whipping post at nearby Helmans Cross could still be seen in its original form, and when the only noise to disturb the peace of a sunny afternoon was the jarring of wagon wheels on the stony road and the plod of the horse that pulled it.

Richard got a job as bailiff to the local squire, Sir John Maryon Wilson, and kept records as he had done in the army, in meticulous fashion. With his upright bearing, his house and his clean and tidy habits, he must have been quite an attraction to local girls. The one who caught him was Jane Westwood of White Roding. They were married when Jimmy was already conceived and he arrived less than 7 months later. That may have been the reason for the marriage having been performed at Great Waltham. As a sergeant of long standing, there is not much doubt that Richard expected to give orders and to see that they were obeyed in double-quick time. It would seem that his domination of Jimmy and his brother Tommy was so absolute that they never really ventured into the world at all. So, when their father died on 7th November, 1890, at the advanced age of 82, they had no-one to direct their lives and they became more withdrawn than ever.

Jimmy was suspicious of his mother and his brother, he felt persecuted, so he decided to build his own private place in the garden to which he could repair whenever he felt the need. He laboured away at building this hut in the grounds of Sawkins, tucked away behind a blackthorn hedge which on the road side had the added protection of the horse pond. Once it was built, Jimmy could be there, silent and secure, watching through a little peephole, just that small section of the world lying beyond the hedge and pond. By 1895 he was only going into Sawkins itself to sleep and to have a meal. Rows with his mother and brother at those times must have contrasted sharply with the peace that this shy, diffident character found in 'New Place' as he called his hut in his diary.

Raleigh Trevelyan, in his book **A Hermit Disclosed**, published in 1960, tells how he found this diary in the attic of Sawkins when living there during World War II. It, and a whole miscellany of papers, had been covered in the interim by a pile of straw and feathers brought in by the omnipresent sparrows. The diary was written in an appalling scrawl, over-written as well in places, but Trevelyan patiently transcribed it; working on it even while he was in the army. Some people would have found it disappointing in its brevity of entries and of its coverage from 24th March, 1895, to 22nd December, 1897, but Trevelyan shows how fascinating it was after much further research.

The pathetic notes show how Jimmy longed for the warmth of human contact which his father's dominating hardness had denied him. He records how, from the secrecy of New Place, he threw presents over the hedge and into the pond for the children he could hear passing. They would rake into their side the apples, nuts, cherries, radishes, flowers or any other item he could find from the garden he tended. Presents for more special people were left hanging from the fir tree by the gate, or lodged upon the fence itself. In return the village boys, as boys the world over, threw stones on the corrugated iron of his roof and ran away to boast of their bravery. Those special presents were for the girls, to whom he wrote occasional notes, getting in reply requests for more presents. Jimmy told his diary when he left the presents out on fence or tree and, after much watching, at what time they were gone, but it seems that he never came face to face with the girls or ever spoke to them - or to those horrid little boys.

It was in June, 1896, that Jimmy went into the house one night to eat his solitary meal - a rabbit pie his mother had left in the oven. It tasted bitter, so he gave it up and let the dog have it. By midnight he found the dog, his favourite spaniel, stiff in death. He was convinced that the rabbit had been poisoned and that the poison was meant for him. He confided to his diary that his brother was out to poison him. From then on he attended to his own meals and became even more withdrawn.

The diary ends in 1897 when he was 40, though he went on living in New Place for 8 more years. During that time those village girls, Edna, Lucie, Susie and Fanny, all in their Victorian finery and through their busy comings and goings were watched from the peephole by the old man they nick named Harry Cinders, who shyly left them presents, which often included small sums of money, much frowned upon by brother Tommy and even, once, at Christmas, ran to a bottle of wine and a cake. In reply he sometimes received a poorly written acknowledgement. For example, Fanny had put a basket on the gate for some cherries, and in it she had written a note on pages of a Sunday paper, which she had left as '... From Miss Fanny as her keepsake, and will always be Miss Fanny Bell. My dear this book come from Miss Fanny Bell and I hope you will give her some stamps as she wanted you to do. You must give me a penny or 2d before I go. I am going soon. And my mother says if you give her something when I am gone, she would take it to me. Whenever you like you must give Mother something to give to me, and some money too, and you may have this for a keepsake. I wish you would give me a watch and then I would always be Miss Fanny Bell. And you will give someone else things when I am gone. You will not care about me then, You must not give anyone else anything, only my mother. She says she will bring me things if you give them to her X X X X." Strangely enough, the paper which was to be the keepsake also advertised watches! It would seem from Trevelyan's research that the artful little hussy did, in fact, get the watch. It must have been these pathetic little notes that gave rise to the later rumour that Jimmy shut himself away from the world through unrequited love.

There were marvellous tales told in the pub and round the village about the hermit and what he got up to. Some people said he lived in an underground burrow, like a wild animal. One man, perhaps the worse for drink, told of a hair-raising sight of the hermit appearing dripping wet in the dead of night from a total immersion in the River Roding. Naughty children were told that the hermit would come for them

Jimmy's mother grew old and infirm and had to be taken to the Workhouse at Dunmow. The two sons could not and did not want to keep on Sawkins, so after much hesitation, for such a transaction was almost beyond their capabilities, they sold it cheaply and bought, rather dearly, a field called Wood Mead, reached only by a track way down on the banks of the Roding. Here Jimmy really isolated himself. He built another hut behind a series of deep ditches that he dug himself and a barricade of barbed wire, corrugated iron and specially planted hedges. Entrance was through a secret system of trapdoors. Brother Tommy set up his own hut at the other end of the field and acted as messenger and go-between for Jimmy's simple wants. The brothers supported themselves, living on the capital accruing from the sale of the house and on the money from sale of hay and other crops in the field. Jimmy also made a small sum from the honey of his beloved bees of which he kept any number of hives.

From this time on, Jimmy was never heard or seen, though because of this, he figured much in the gossip of the village. Tommy would report on his health and welfare and would buy him seeds, wire, flour and so on. It should be appreciated that Jimmy was already 50 years old when he moved to this primitive and solitary retreat. The local papers and even the **Daily Mail** noted this move, but an opportunist journalist revived interest in the brothers 23 years later in 1927. As Trevelyan writes: "... according to the correspondent September 5th 1927 was exactly the fiftieth anniversary of Jimmy's decision to become a hermit - a decision which had been made 'on the impulse of the moment' when he was aged 20. The very insistence on the precise day of the vow, in all that clap-trap, was enough to prove that the date was pure invention."

Trevelyan also comments: "... I realised that here was the source of the whole scurrilous, exaggerated legend of the vow, that had brought Jimmy and Tommy so much misery in their old age." The correspondent had the idea of getting past Jimmy's defences to ask him for a 'message to the outside world'. He negotiated all the traps and tapped the door and looked in at the window. All he got for his pains was a view of Jimmy, bearded long and white, lying in his crude orange-box bed and crying tremulously, "Stranger, you cannot come here. Please,

please, go away, stranger."

The villagers could not have helped the journalist into Jimmy's den, for the only people to have seen him since his move in 1904 had been his brother, Mrs Sales, a villager who called occasionally in his later life to do washing and other little services for him, and the Vicar who had once had to be called in to get Jimmy to sign the forms to assure him of an old-age pension - much-needed money that Tommy could collect.

It was through this latest news coverage that Fanny, the flighty village girl, now a matronly East-Ender, was persuaded by a publican to visit the hermit, to succeed where the newspaper had failed in getting the poor old man to talk. Off she went, perhaps with an eye to getting more out of Jimmy in remembrance of the old association across the pond. She thought he might have secreted away a lot of money - a very welcome reward for scrambling through the wire and the mud to effect a reunion. Her approach was spotted by Tommy who immediately set out on a two-mile walk to ask for help in turning her out. But she was successful, she got her name in the paper and a couple of hours in the hermit's dark and dismal shanty.

Of money, though, there was none. She returned frustrated and deflated - Jimmy looked less like a hermit than like a dirty, ill-kempt, inadequate old man. Wood Mead returned to the absolute peace of the countryside where the loudest noise was the activity of his buzzing bees.

For 15 more years the ageing hermit kept to his hut. The only other intrusion on his peace was the explosion of one of the first bombs to be dropped in this neighbourhood, in 1940. It was small, but it landed only yards from the hut, blowing down the corrugated fence and barbed wire. The boggy ground absorbed most of the shock. Jimmy did not realise his escape, simply remarking to Mrs Sales when she enquired after him next day, that he had heard tractors working all night. In January,1942, Jimmy died, his death unnoticed in a world of death and destruction. On that snowy day he was discovered in his hut, a thin, undernourished 84-year-old man whose only clothing was a tattered shirt and trousers. The village policeman and the undertaker's assistant had to carry the pathetic remains of the Canfield hermit through deep snow to the ambulance at the end of the track 800 yards away.

His brother Tommy shall have the last word in the form of the statement he made to the police: "For the past 36 years I have lived next door to the deceased: he was a hermit and lived alone, and he has lived all on his own for the last 60 years.

"He used to lock himself in his hut and I used to take him a few things for his meals... At about 4 p.m. on Saturday, January 17th, 1942, I saw the dead body of Alexander James Mason, aged 84 years; I identify that as of my brother."

The next scene is set in Gestingthorpe - not a particularly noteworthy Essex village. Even the official guide to the district can only work up a certain tepid enthusiasm: "... Gestingthorpe village lines the road for over a mile from Belchamp Brook in the north to the junction with the Hedingham-Sudbury road in the south." That, at least, gives us a geographical location and the guide continues, "There are many old cottages of great charm and notable houses include Over Hall, which stands surrounded by trees opposite the church..."

It is at Over Hall, now better known as Gestingthorpe Hall, that we remember a boy who had a happy childhood here. Obviously, living in such a house, he was not a poor boy; his great disadvantage was frailty of health. Before he reached his teens he had three times been sent on voyages to South Africa in attempts to improve his constitution and his resistance to infection. This boy, Lawrence Edward Grace Oates, was born in 1880 at Putney, in the days when the horse was still the king of the road: Edward grew up with a ruling passion for horses. When they moved to Gestingthorpe, horses in the stable were an absolute necessity, simply to keep in touch with the outside world. When Lawrence came back from those long sea trips, he would have headed straight for the stables behind Over Hall to greet his beloved animals. Sent to Eton, he lasted just two years before catching pneumonia and so being taken away for good.

Growth brought strength; in the Essex open air, the youth revelled in a new-found vitality born more of character than of external stimulation. He showed that character when, as a lad of 18, he joined his brother in the purchase of a boat, the 18 ton yawl, **Saunterer**. He loved the sea and sailing and cheerfully faced the challenge of a storm, though he suffered much from sea-sickness. In his choice of career, however, his love of horses and his horsemanship pointed him towards a commission in a cavalry regiment. First, though, he had to serve an apprenticeship for two years with the West Yorkshire Militia. Then, just 20 years old, Lawrence was delighted to be posted to the Inniskilling Dragoons as a humble subaltern. He had been so afraid that the Boer War would be over before he could get out there to exercise his youthful enthusiasm and do his patriotic duty.

It was not until December, 1900 that a regimental detachment of 50 men and 3 officers, accompanied by the regimental band, stepped ashore in Cape Town. Within a matter of days they were sent into action in a local skirmish; Oates' reward was promotion to Lieutenant. He moved on, with his men, to join the column under Colonel Pearson making its way to the relief of Aberdeen. It ran into trouble with Boer guerillas who were inflicting more casualties than the column could sustain. Three patrols, each of 15 men, were sent out to draw the fire and quell the snipers. Lieutenant Oates was selected to lead one of these patrols. His men soon came up with the Boers and took them on, but then found themselves completely tied down by the enemy's superior fire power.

There was nothing that Oates could do other than care for his men as best he could and make sure that their arms did not fall into enemy hands. He directed each man, when he had fired his last bullet, to creep away under cover of the bush, back to the safety of the column and the camp. Twice the Boers, waving the customary white flag of a safe passage, sent over a messenger demanding the patrol's surrender, but Oates made them understand they were there to fight, not to give in. After four hours Oates had got all his men away, though early on he had received a bullet in the thigh that had broken the bone. Through his masterly control, the Boers, who had at one time penetrated to within 20 yards, had finally to give up their attempt to capture the patrol. They did not even get a single rifle. Young Oates had been injured at 10 in the morning, the horse ambulance trundled along to pick him up at 6.30 that evening.

The action gave Oates his nickname in the army - 'No surrender Oates'. A period of convalescence followed, with his mother at Gestingthorpe. She celebrated his return in the restoration of the church bells, the fifth and sixth of which are inscribed "In gratitude to God for the safe return with honour of my beloved son from the dangers of war in South Africa." No doubt he was able to enjoy more horse-riding, hunting and steeplechasing, as he recouped his health before returning to the front and his regiment. Not until 31st October did they say goodbye to the Cape and by then Lawrence had been awarded the Queen's Medal and 5 clasps for his acts of gallantry. The regiment travelled round the globe, to India and, since peace reigned at last there, life was a rather boring anti-climax. Oates reacted with customary spirit, arranging the gathering together at Gestingthorpe of a motley collection of hounds and had them sent out to Mhow, the Inniskillings base. There he organised the strangest hunts, with officers dressed in a variety of clothes, and good fun was had by all. That fun soon dispersed in the mind-sapping heat and the enforced inactivity.

So Lawrence Oates was in exactly the right frame of mind to grasp at the opportunity offered by the news that the famous Captain Robert Falcon Scott was looking for a team to conquer the South Pole, to tread where no man had ever trodden before. A world of whirling snow and biting cold; what a striking contrast! Lawrence wrote off at once, asking to be included. Scott wanted to know what he could offer; Oates was able to show that, if dogs were to be used, he had managed a pack of hounds and, if it was to be horse to haul the sleds, well, he had studied how Tibetans used them in their lofty mountain villages. No doubt his decorations for gallantry were also noticed by Scott who considered this brave, fit, strong young man as just the person he wanted. Oates had got special leave in England for the interview and the War Office extended his leave of absence to include his 'extra-regimental employ with the British Antarctic Expedition'.

His special assignment in the team was the responsibility for the transport and care of the dogs and ponies to be used in the extreme temperatures of Antarctica. Oates was so thrilled with the prospect of going to the South Pole that he even plucked up the courage to ask Scott if he might be given the chance to go with that small body of men who would press on from the last supply base to the very Pole itself.

In June, 1910, the expedition's ship **Terra Nova** set sail from Cardiff on the sea journey to the icy continent. The ship was built for strength to resist the ice's powerful embrace rather than for speed and took 5 months to get to Port Chalmers in New Zealand, from where they were to jump off to South Victoria Land. Before they left, however, Scott had a telegram from fellow-explorer Amundsen. He was supposed to be on an Arctic expedition, but now he announced he was going to head for the South Pole. So the race was on and the honour of England and of Norway was at stake. As far as young Oates was concerned the news added to the excitement and redoubled his spirit of patriotism.

The **Terra Nova** set forth, loaded with supplies for the great attempt; there was no question of sending back for things forgotten. Oates knew that he would have to take the greatest care of those 33 sled-dogs and 19 tough little Manchurian ponies who would have to endure more than a month of the roughest seas. For all his ministrations a dog was soon lost, drowned when a heavy sea washed over the ship. A pony died, possibly of seasickness. The weather eased and they were able to eat a good Christmas dinner with the ship decorated overall, as they drifted practically icebound.

On the first day of the New Year they had their first sight of the frozen land, the peaks of the mountains a hundred miles away could be seen clearly. Once safely anchored offshore work went on under appalling difficulties to build strong winter quarters. Then expeditions with the ponies hauling supplies were made further and further out along the projected route to dump caches of essential supplies for the return journey from the Pole. The **Terra Nova** had to move out before it was caught in the ice. One of its last communications to Scott was the news that Amundsen had already got ashore in the Bay of Whales, 60 miles nearer the Pole.

This was bad news for the Englishmen, but winter was closing in and neither party would now be able to do anything but sit it out until the permanent darkness and the bitter blizzards relaxed their grip on this inhospitable land. Scott's men made themselves as comfortable as possible; their luxuries, landed from the ship, included a piano, a gramophone and plenty of books. They also took it in turn to give lectures. Oates, of course, talked about horses, and he was as busy as any member of the team, for he still had the dogs and ponies to look after. He had already been upset by the failure of the ponies in the staking out of supplies. By the time they had returned to base, seven of them had died from one cause or another, so their use on the dash to the Pole itself was now somewhat in question. Scott intended that they should pull the sleds 400 miles to the Beardmore Glacier and then be shot. From there the small group going on to the Pole would haul their gear themselves and, with the benefit of the caches of food, return fairly easily under their own steam. Oates must have had very mixed feelings about the disposal of the ponies, for his daily life since going aboard ship had been dedicated to keeping the unhappy animals alive.

The first appearance of the sun on 23rd August brought great excitement in the preparation for the task ahead. The men, cramped together in the snow-bound hut, had to get really fit again for the exacting journey before them. Then, so many things went wrong that it seemed as if the venture was doomed from the outset. The party should have moved off by the end of September if they were to beat the return of unbroken night, but through accident and argument they did not set out until 1st November. Consequently, they ran into weather so quixotic in its extremes that they were utterly frustrated. One day they would make progress in brilliant, searingly cold sunshine and then, for days on end, they were buried in their tents by the blinding blizzards blowing as if the end of the world had come. After a fortnight of intense effort they had covered just 130 miles.

Now they were to find that Scott was wrong in relying on ponies in this wilderness of ice. The wretched creatures could not cope with the climate of the Great Ice Barrier and one by one they had to be put out of their misery. Oates loved them, they had been his especial care all through; he was willing them to pull the sleds through to the Glacier, but their stumbling and struggling and dying were only adding to an already dangerous delay. As they approached the Glacier Scott made up his mind and gave the order that they were all to be shot and Oates was to be the executioner. What a test of character! Oates obeyed immediately. "I thank you, Titus", said Scott, using his nickname. The slaughter was noted in the name of the stop they made - Shambles Camp.

Once on the Glacier a cache of supplies was dropped, then the remaining dogs were sent back down the line and 12 men carried on hauling three sleds carrying more than a ton between them, looking to make two more caches on the Glacier, with a journey of 500 miles still before them. The team was to be reduced to 8 when they had traversed the Glacier, and Oates was very glad that, when the time of choice came, and Scott wanted him to go on. Yet there was little to be happy about. Christmas Day, 1911, was spent hauling one of the party, Lashley, out of a deep crevasse, where he was swinging at the end of the climbing rope uniting them all, and so nearly taking them all down with him. The weather improved for a time and, as the old year ebbed away, they were up to their schedule, having achieved an average of 15 miles a day. With 150 miles to go, three of the team were considered too ill to push on, they would only be a serious handicap in what was becoming a test of survival itself. Reluctantly they were sent back while Scott and four trusty companions headed on with just one month's food supply.

As the group stumbled on to complete their mission, Scott, in his diary, summed up his opinion of his comrades' characters, including Oates, of whom he wrote: "Oates had his invaluable period with the ponies. Now he is a foot slogger and goes hard the whole time, does his share of camp work, and stands the hardship as well as any of us. I would not like to be without him either." There were 70 miles to go, but blizzards were making progress so difficult in the intense cold. By now every man was suffering, but still they persevered. When they were in sight of their goal, just 27 miles short of the Pole, on 16th January, 1912, they came across, in that white land of untrodden snow, the tracks of dogs, sleds and men. They studied them and saw quite clearly that they had first headed south and then returned north. There was only one explanation - Amundsen had passed this way to the Pole and had come back on his victorious journey to fame and glory.

How hard it must have been for those utterly exhausted Englishmen to take such a blow to their hopes of planting their country's flag first at the South Pole. They could only swallow their disappointment and struggle on to keep faith with their colleagues. They reached the Pole and found in a tent left by the Norwegians a note addressed to Captain Scott, asking him to take a letter and deliver it to King Haakon in case the Norwegian party was overtaken by disaster on the way back. It was a terrible anticlimax, but they rallied, planted their flag, took photographs and set themselves to the journey back.

Oates, when he set out, was, at 32 years old, a fit man, but the terrible hardship of the expedition had sapped his strength. Evans, too, was finding the prospect of the 900 miles return journey daunting in the extreme. A following wind at first gave them encouragement, then cruelly taunted them, turned against them, searing through the thicknesses of their clothes and boots. Oates was suffering severely from frost-bitten feet, but he plodded on. It was poor Evans who was delaying their progress; he collapsed repeatedly and finally became delerious. They fixed him up as best they could with their limited medical outfit and got going again, but he fell so far behind as actually to pass out of sight. It was Oates who was asked to go back and help him on. Oates did so at once, though the extra journey must have aggravated his frostbite. He struggled with him back to camp and then had to crouch beside him while he died during the night.

Now it was Oates himself who became the drag on the long march. "Poor Titus is our greatest handicap", wrote Scott. Yet he would not give in; he struggled so hard to keep up. The cold grew even more intense and his frostbitten limbs could not respond to the demands even of his friends' slow progress in the dreadful conditions. He asked Scott to leave him behind in his sleeping bag, so that they could press on to base and to safety, but, of course, they would not hear of it. Lawrence Oates knew what he had to do. He was quite at the end of his physical strength. He talked to his friends of his mother and his home in Essex, of his concern for his regiment and finally settled to sleep, hoping that during the night he would die and no longer hinder the tired band's final push to the cache of food that spelled rest, refreshment and recouping of energy and hope. Let Scott's diary carry on the story: "He was a brave soul. He slept through the night, hoping not to wake, but he woke in the morning. It was blowing a blizzard. Oates said, 'I am just going outside, I may be some time.' We knew he was walking to his death; but though we tried to dissuade him, we knew it was the act of a brave man and an English gentle man." It was his birthday, 17th March, 1912.

As the world knows, his sacrifice was unavailing. The trio left struggled on to within 11 miles of that cache at One Ton Camp, then the weather closed in on them completely and they died together in their pitiful little tent. That was on 29th March. Their bodies were found by a search party on 12th

ESSEX PRIDE

November following, but no trace of the gallant Oates was ever found. A cairn and a cross were set up to mark the locality in which he died.

Thomas Clarkson considerably altered the face of Chelmsford, gave employment to thousands and spread the name of the county town throughout the world.

He was a Lancashire lad, born on 24th September, 1863, in Salford, and brought up in the Manchester area, a great place for a boy with a passion for engines at a time when steam was king and British-made machinery operated in every clime. Thomas was fascinated by these mechanical marvels and that childhood 'craze' developed into his life's work.

At the age of 13 he was apprenticed to an engineering firm. When he was 21 he won the award of a senior Whitworth Scholarship and, in the same year, a National Science Scholarship that took him on a 3-year course at the Royal College of Science in London. So he qualified to be a Lecturer in Metallurgy, teaching at King's College for 2 years. Then his restless mind drove him on to travel throughout Europe and the United States. He returned to take up a Senior Lectureship at the School of Mines, but, while teaching others, he was still anxious to learn from his own experiments. The cliche, 'a born inventor' could honestly be applied to Mr Clarkson.

He was only 24 when he filed his first patent - for a separator of various minerals using a centrifuge - and many others followed, including a sifting machine, a drafting maching and a system of ball bearings. Two patents he filed in 1895, for a condenser and for a 'light, steam car' were signposts to his trend towards his total preoccupation with steam traction. The steam car was revolutionary in design. Thomas made all the parts and assembled them in a workshop near the College. It was hard work, lecturing during the day and manufacturing his own car at night; and the car came first, so Thomas looked round for more suitable premises and found them with Herbert Capel, gas engine manufacturer of Dalston. He promptly gave up his job to work solely for the Clarkson and Capel Steam Car Syndicate.

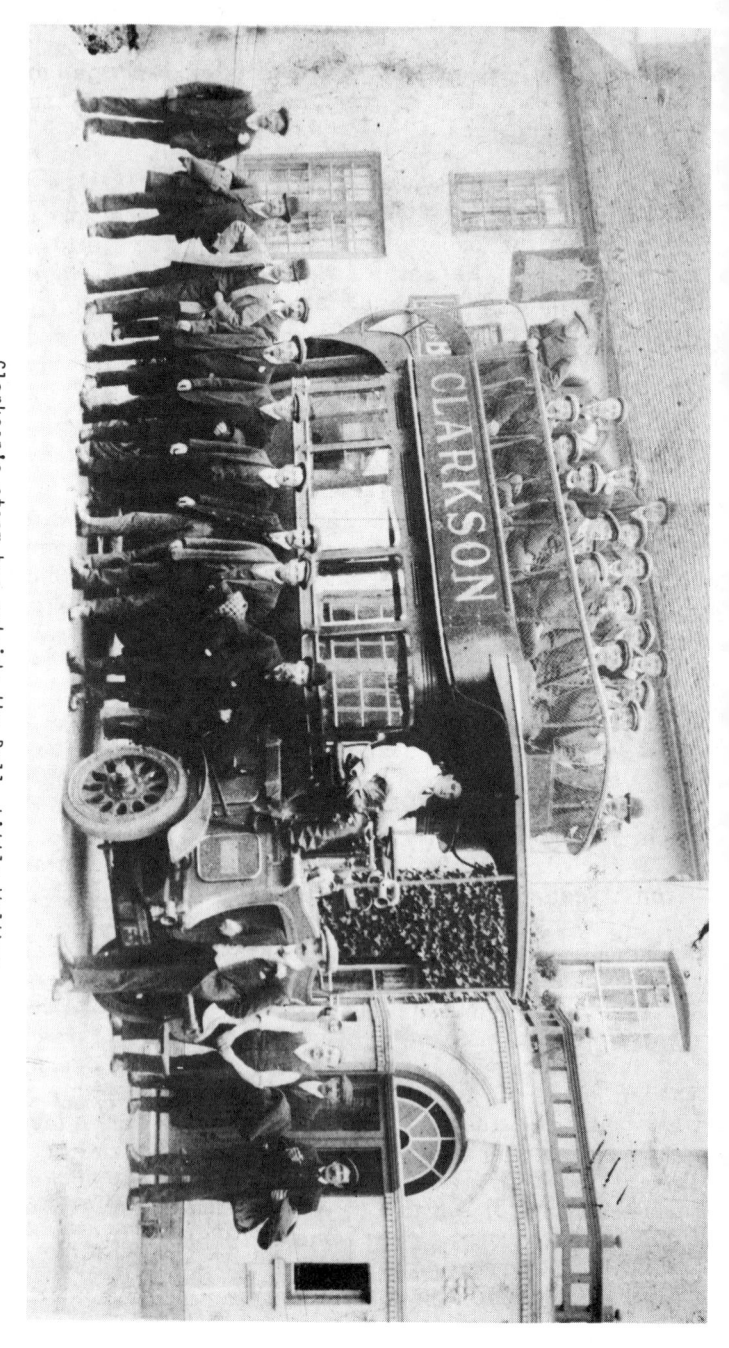

Clarkson's steam bus outside the Bell, Little Waltham

Then, during 1898, Thomas built his very own 'steam landau' to put on show at the horseless carriage exhibition in Richmond Park. He had to continue on his own after that, because Capel died of typhoid contracted when they went to the States together to look after their patent interests in 1899.

It meant that Thomas had to look for new premises, and he decided this time to work on his own, to such good effect that, in the same year that his partner died, he sent his prototype steam lorry to the second Liverpool trials. By 1902 he had found the premises he wanted - in Chelmsford. There had been a factory on the site from as early as 1815 when John Bewley established his iron foundry there. Then Crompton's (later Crompton, Parkinson & Co.) used the site until their factory was burned down in 1895, when they moved to larger premises off the Writtle Road. The foundry on the site was, however, continued by Colonel Crompton's old associate, T H P Dennis, a hydraulics engineer, until his retirement in 1902 and Clarkson's appearance on the scene.

Now Thomas got down to the serious business of manufacturing his steam car in numbers, calling his firm Clarkson, Ltd., and his prototype chassis the 'Chelmsford'. It was designed to support 'a substantial, roomy steam brougham suitable for the conveyance in comfort of eight passengers with their luggage over long journeys'. He had few buyers, though, because petrol-driven internal combustion engines were now all the rage, even though they were jerky, noisy and smelly compared with the elegance of the steam car. At an exhibition, however, it caught the eye of 'a party of persons from Torquay' who were anxious to start an omnibus service in that locality. They wanted to know if Clarkson could revise the design to increase the number of passengers. In a very few weeks he had plans for a new model drawn up - and accepted.

The first new steam bus was driven from the factory in Chelmsford straight down to Exeter, where the purchasers were picked up, and then on to Torquay, arriving in perfect working order. Successful operation over routes around Torquay led to an order for eight more and they were all produced by Easter,

1905. They gained such a good reputation that within a few months orders came in from all parts of the United Kingdom and from places overseas as varied as Australia, India, New Zealand and Barbados.

At this time the total staff was no more than 50 and the factory urgently needed modernising and re-equipping to maintain a level of production sufficient to meet such a demand. Having achieved the expansion, Clarkson realised that he would have to secure many more orders if he was to stay in business at this level. He was quick to appreciate that the main user of such buses would be the transport company operating in a great metropolis like London where horse-transport was just waiting to be improved upon. Thomas persuaded the London General Omnibus Company to order a 14-seater, single-decker bus for £605. Trials on various routes from October to June, 1905, showed that it was running at a loss. Clarkson cleverly suggested that profit could be made if the single-decker was replaced by a double-decker, taking twice the number of passengers. His arguments were persuasive. He immediately designed such a vehicle and sold twelve to the Company - and a further 25 to its rival the London Road Car Company. With big concerns showing such confidence in the steam bus, orders followed from smaller transport operators in the London area.

Chelmsford folk got accustomed to the sight of brand new steam buses moving powerfully down the road to London. Work went well in the factory until the middle of 1907, when the flow of orders dried up. The trouble was that Chelmsford-built buses lasted forever: there was no built-in 'obsolescence' about a Clarkson steam bus. The problem of keeping the workmen employed was temporarily solved by producing items for other types of steam engineering while Thomas worked night and day to design a new light-weight chassis conforming to the stringent regulations then imposed. He had it ready by June, 1908, but orders were slow. Yet Thomas did not despair: he looked out for other business and came upon an unusual opportunity.

It was at this time that the reform of the army brought the introduction of the Territorials and they needed exercises and manoeuvres, during which they required reliable transport to get them quickly to the battle area. Thomas put himself out to be pleasant to the officers of the Essex Yeomanry at their Chelmsford depot. He captured Captain Wenley's imagination with his steaming monsters and he declared at an army conference that he could get troops from the Chelmsford depot down to the banks of the Crouch in one and a half hours. Senior officers challenged him to prove it in a test arranged for Sunday, 6th December, 1908. There was such a bustle that morning at the Territorial Headquarters in Chelmsford as Clarkson steam buses embarked 128 men, along with officers and journalists, all in the pouring rain, at two minutes past ten exactly. At nine minutes past eleven they all tumbled out at Latchingdon, 14 miles away and in one minute were formed up ready for action.

The Commanding Officer, Colonel R B Colvin was so impressed that he hired the buses to take the Yeomanry to their camp at Sudbury in the following year. For this occasion and in the hope of procuring further military contracts, Thomas had the double-deckers completely repainted, changed the name blazoned on their sides from 'Chelmsford' to 'National' and included patriotic slogans, such as 'Wake up, England!'. But the War Office was slow to make up its mind and, while they dithered, work withered, so Thomas had to act quickly. With Colonel Colvin as a fellow director, he formed his own London transport company, calling it the National Steam Car Company, on 19th June, 1909. With his usual flair for publicity, Thomas put on a special inaugural run on 30th October, 1909, at which '... several contingents of Boy Scouts were also present'. The proper service started on 2nd November with just four steamers operating from one of the great arches of the viaduct of the London and South Western Railway. It made a profit, so more buses were made and routes were extended. Clarkson overcame the lack of demand on Sundays by introducing 'Sunday Specials' to take Londoners to popular picnic spots like Hampstead Heath. By the end of 1910 there were 20 buses on the streets proudly proclaiming the

'National' service. The Chelmsford factory was, thankfully, very busy again. The company prospered and was re-constituted to take over the bus service of the Great Eastern railway operating out of Chelmsford, where the garage was, again, an archway in the viaduct overlooking the present bus station. So the National Bus Company flourished, increasing the number of passengers from 6,000,000 in 1911 to 24,000,000 in 1913.

This profitable venture gave Thomas time and money to go back to his passion for invention and improvement in his battle against the petrol driven engine. From the use of paraffin as the heating agent he moved on to coke, even though it necessitated an entirely new type of boiler, and built a chassis to prove it would operate far more cheaply. The Clarkson lorry earned trophies on its test run from London to Brighton, but there was trouble with fumes, and the hoped-for interest from transport firms was not forthcoming. In 1914 Thomas became Chairman and Managing Director of the firm, just as war broke out and dividends began to fall. This was not so much the effect of the war, but because Thomas' concentration on research for development of steam transport was eating into the profits. The war did, in fact, bring some work for the Chelmsford factory, in making shell cases and boilers for army bath-caravans. In these interests the government gave a grant for the extension of the works.

The joint Managing Director and the board struggled to make the firm profitable after losses in 1918 of nearly £20,000, but Thomas was so absorbed in his research that he was metaphorically shunted into a siding and his cash flow was severely limited. One hard decision to be made was the withdrawal from the London transport scene, where they could no longer be competitive. The 'National Steamers' in all their white and gold elegance returned powerfully and quietly to the Chelmsford works, where they were dismantled. The board went ahead with petrol driven buses in the provinces and in one year made a profit of £22,000. No wonder that a board meeting minute reported: "Mr Clarkson was still experimenting with paraffin and creosote as fuels for a steam chassis and that there was nothing further to report thereon."

In 1920, while the firm expanded, old Thomas, still studying steam at the Chelmsford works, was simply shown as a line on the debit side of the business with the Steam car account credited with £61,000 for the value of the now useless chassis, a lot of superseded spare parts and the doubtful value of all those Clarkson patents. At the A.G.M. in 1921, the Chairman announced that Thomas Clarkson had left the Company "... and from now on no further expenses will be incurred by this company on his account..." The Chelmsford works were closed, lease transferred and machinery sold. The National Company gave up bus-making and concentrated on bus services. Yet, in that same year, on 6th January, Thomas Clarkson was reading a paper to the Chelmsford Engineering Society on 'Motor Transport Economics' and another paper in October. His character is summed up in an article in the **Gentleman's journal** of December, 1907: "It is said that the busy man has the most time. Mr Clarkson is an excellent example of the truth of this dictum. He has proved himself a good citizen of his adopted town [of Chelmsford], and was last year returned to the Council at the head of the poll, yet, with all his varied engagements, he still finds time to contribute many valuable papers on engineering subjects to the advancement of science. His thorough grasp of his subject gives his writings great weight... It is such men as Mr Clarkson that have made the history of the advancement of the motor industry in England read like eleven years of miracles."

Such, however, is the fickleness of human memory that, for all the work that Clarkson did, all his inventive genius, all the work and wages he gave to Chelmsford and Essex people for 16 years, his death has passed unrecorded in all the local histories - his marvellous innovations overlooked in the passing of the age of steam.

It is 60 years since Lord Peter Wimsey, the handsome, rich, amateur sleuth, became a national character whose exploits were followed, through translation, by detective story addicts all over the world. And it is as recent as 1977 that the famous authoress was being enthused over yet again as the Dorothy L Sayers Historical and Literary Society held a 'Talking of Dorothy L Sayers...' evening at Spring Lodge, Witham, where she lived for some 27 years. The house she lived in, saved from destruction by Essex County Council, was restored as two residences and opened formally in November, 1975, with the unveiling of a plaque reading: "Dorothy L Sayers 1893-1957, novelist, theologian, and Dante Scholar lived here." But it is her detective stories that remain in print and by which she is known by the general public.

In her fifties, when she came to Witham, Dorothy was a large, not to say a fat, woman, who walked about the town in the most casual of clothes, sometimes forgetfully sallying out to the grocer's with her apron still tied about her. It was hard to believe that this was the very famous writer, who would probably have preferred to be remembered for her writings on Christian topics.

She was born on 13 June, 1893, daughter of the Reverend Henry Sayers, headmaster of Christ Church College Choir School, Oxford, and his wife Helen, a vivacious woman with a strong sense of humour. When Dorothy was 4 the family moved to the living of Bluntisham-cum-Earith in Huntingdonshire, on the edge of the Fens. Here Dorothy was surrounded with the loving care of parents, nurse, cook, 3 maids and a manservant in a well-run, happy household. Yet she was a lonely child, for at home she was an only child, and in the village she was cut off by her class from the rough-and-tumble fun in which the schoolchildren joined. She was not one of them, for she was educated at home by parents and governess. Her friends were found in her dolls, in her toy monkeys, Jacko and Jocko, and in the characters in the books she read voraciously. She could read by the time she was 4, and took to Latin and French with ease and enthusiasm. At 7 years old she had started her own imaginative writing and by her mid-teens was turning out witty and technically perfect verse. Not until then did she find a pleasurable connection with a fellow spirit of her own generation. Her cousin, Ivy Shrimpton, was five years her senior, but that was an advantage in that Dorothy could call her a true friend and, at the same time, look up to her a little as a grown-up. It was while Ivy was staying with her in 1907 that Dorothy showed her imaginative power in staging, in her 'schoolroom', a dramatisation of **The Threee Musketeers**, in which everybody in the rectory had to take a part. For a whole year she lived the character, writing 'Cavalier poems with swaggering choruses' - a 14-year-old still deeper in romance than in reality. She showed too, in writing to Ivy, that she could turn out very acceptable verses in perfect French. Such letters could run to twenty pages, with decorations and doodles on every page; works of art that caused C S Lewis to call her one of the great letter-writers. She was developing her literary talent, and her desire to shrug off company and relatives who wanted to be helpful at this time was the evidence of her artistic temperament. But for Ivy she reserved a special place in her affection, a place to prove of great help to her in later life.

She was $15\frac{1}{2}$ when she went away to school at Salisbury. The family surely breathed a sigh of relief, for Dorothy's enquiring mind must have taxed their own knowledge. It was a very difficult time for her, a tubby girl on the verge of womanhood who had never been to school before; but she surprised her teachers with her inspired use of language in her compositions, and eventually obtained a very good Higher Certificate. Then, in February, 1911, she became gravely ill with measles followed by pneumonia, and all her hair fell out. She had to go back to school and face all the additional cruel teasing on that score, because she needed to study hard for the Gilchrist Scholarship that she hoped would take her into the wonderful world of Somerville College, Oxford. Though she had to admit defeat at the hands of her mocking schoolmates, she continued her study back in the rectory and her natural cleverness, combined with her intense desire to reach the Mecca of university life, took her through.

College was everything she hoped it would be. She made friends with women intellectually her match, especially those who had banded together to form the Mutual Admiration Society. The qualification for membership was the writing of an original work, to be read out at the meeting. It is significant that Dorothy chose to postulate a conversation between the Three Wise Men as her contribution. She was estimated by later literati as easily the most brilliant of that clever coterie.

Dorothy's spirit shines out of a letter written to her university friend while she was on vacation in 1913. She said that her usual technique of 'vehemently disagreeing with everybody' did not arouse her family to heated reply as it did the M.A.S.: "... I miss our loud-voiced arguments... hang it all, what were tongues made for?" She really enjoyed the give and take of a rumbustious debate. This is borne out by her brilliant contribution to the Balliol debate on the motion 'That the educated classes of the present day show a sad lack of enthusiasm'. That charge certainly could not be levelled at Dorothy! One of her letters contains the phrase, "... I love being enthusiastic in a whole mass of people..."

She was taking her Finals when the men under graduates were off to the Great War. She worked very hard and obtained a First Class Honours degree in modern languages, with emphasis on French. There were no jobs in the offing which had the least appeal, so Dorothy had to go back to a home of elderly parents, a terrible anticlimax to Oxford. She spent her time putting together a collection of her poems. Her determination to get into print was asserting itself. Then the opportunity of a post as teacher of Modern languages at Hull high School for Girls was gratefully seized and a further cause for excitement was the appearance in print, in 1916, of her poems called **Op.1**, published by Blackwell's in what they called their 'Series of Young Poets Unknown to Fame'. Further success followed in acceptances by magazines and in a poetry competition in the **Saturday Westminster Review.**

It was at this time that she changed her job, perhaps through her father's mediation, and went to work for Blackwell's in London as a proof reader. Life opened out for her, including a couple of romantic encounters. Living in lodgings gave her greater freedom, she made so many friends, was given a rise in pay and moved into better rooms on the strength of it. At 23 she had not had an intimate affair with a man; her life was a vaccillation between her religion, her poetry, and her concern over what she considered was her lack of sexual attraction. She went off on a tangent, to France, as an assistant to a teacher called Eric Whelpton, whom she had met as a neighbour in rooms. After a couple of years there she contracted mumps. It may have been in the free time of her convalescence that she showed an interest in detective stories with a brilliant analysis of Sexton Blake, carried out in mock, literary-historical style.

She sensed that this was the section of writing and publishing where there was money to be made and asked Whelpton to go in with her, but he was not interested. So, from September, 1920, she came back to London, produced a film script of **Blood and Sand** by Ibanez, for which she was never paid, and then suffered a succession of disappointments in jobs and rooms. In a chance conversation her friend, Muriel Jaeger, told her that she was writing a novel in her spare time. Dorothy declared that she would never be able to apply herself long enough to get to the end, yet, when she was at home on holiday in July, 1920, she did apply herself and the debonair Lord Peter Wimsey walked into her book, and into her life. By October she was reporting that the book was nearly ready for typing. James Brabazon in his **Dorothy L Sayers**, sums up very neatly: "And so, mysteriously, was born Lord Peter Death Bredon Wimsey, second son of the Duke of Denver; without whom Dorothy L Sayers would surely never have made any discernible mark on the mind of the public at large."

The book, **Whose Body?** was typed at her father's expense for she was at a very low ebb financially.

She found new rooms in Great James Street

that she occupied for 20 years as her fame and fortune dramatically increased. She also obtained a well-paid job with Benson's, the advertising agents, just ten minutes from her flat, and was involved in a passionate affair with John Cournos, a refugee Russian Jew. So, 30 years old, in 1923, Dorothy was riding the crest of a wave of happiness. The affair foundered, but Dorothy wrote most mysteriously at the end of the year to tell her mother she would be coming home for Christmas with a man and a motor-bike. The man, whose name we shall never know, was what might be called a healthy change from the suffocating, philosophical self-satisfaction of John Cournos. The man was unliterary, but practical and positive and good with cars. He was just fun to be with. By May, 1923, Dorothy knew she was pregnant by him and they were both very fed up about it. There was nobody in whom she could confide; she certainly could not tell her parents.

At this time **Whose Body?** was a great help with the royalties it produced to relieve her of financial worries about the impending arrival. As its father would not marry her, Dorothy had to make arrangements for the future of her baby. She wrote to her cousin Ivy, already fostering children as a means of livelihood, and asked her to take on a nameless infant whom she heard had no father. Ivy was pleased to oblige, though she was not let into the secret of its true identity. So, at 30 years old, Dorothy was delivered of a male child who was handed over to Ivy as soon as possible. Even her friends at Benson's never knew the reason for Dorothy's brief absence and she resumed her life of copywriting and authorship as if the man had been a ghost.

As her life got back to normal, and with a good salary coming in, Dorothy took pleasure in eating and drinking - she loved the taste of beer and the atmosphere of a pub. She was a loud, large lady full of enthusiasm whatever the subject in hand. She was writing again, several short stories and the opening of **Clouds of Witnesses**, that appeared in 1926, when the next man came into her life - and she married him. Oswald Atherton (as he called himself) Fleming had been married before but was divorced. A Captain in the R.A.S.C. in the War, he was gassed and shell-shocked, but recovered to resume his career as a journalist. It was not apparently a marriage of kindred spirits on an intellectual plane, and it may have descended into a kind of necessary monotony, but it must be said that during it, between 1926 and 1937, Dorothy wrote twelve more detective stories with Wimsey as the central character. It is facinating to think that at least five of them would have been thought out, and much of them written, in Dorothy's 'cottage' at Witham.

Meanwhile her success at Benson's continued in association with John Gilroy. She composed a verse that went round the world and down the years and must have sold an ocean of stout. Older people still remember it with a certain affection: under a picture of a bird with its beak cantilevered out over two glasses of the dark liquid there was written:

"If he can say as you can
Guinness is good for you,
How grand to be a Toucan,
Just think what Toucando."

As her royalties and her reputation increased, her husband Mac's diminished and illness in 1928 really set him back, and set back also Dorothy's plan to bring her little son into the family home. Then, in September, 1928, her father died and she had to find a home for her mother and her aunt. It was Mac who found the suitable house, and Dorothy wrote to her mother that 'Sunnyside', Newland Street, Witham, Essex, was to be her new address, for she and Mac had bought it from the Gardners. By Christmas the move had been made and Mrs Sayers and Aunt Mabel were sufficiently settled in to welcome Dorothy and Mac for the holiday. Mrs Sayers only lived a few more months, dying in August, 1929, so now there was the problem of what to do with the house. Dorothy's reputation as an author had appreciated to the extent that she now received a regular commission to concentrate on writing, so that she could even give up her lucrative work at Benson's. She decided that Witham would be just the place to hide away, to write without interruption. It would be a weekend retreat while she kept up her London connections, then it could become her dwelling-place, reversing roles with her London flat. Now she was a free-lance author, there were no 9-to-5 hours for her, she just worked all the hours she could, and enjoyed every minute of it. The following year she bought the adjoining house, Chantry Cottage, from Miss Vaux for £650 and joined the two internally with archways through the wall to connect sitting rooms and joined the front bedrooms to make one large library.

Though she could not by any means be said to have joined in the life of Witham, her presence was noted with a certain awe and respect for her fame. About the town she dressed casually, but for special occasions she would look splendidly elaborate, as when she went off to London for dinners of the Detection Club. Though it started as a simple, friendly, informal meeting of writers of detective stories, for Dorothy it became a deadly serious occasion with special rituals, growing out of spontaneous improvisation, which she insisted should be studiously observed with almost Masonic solemnity.

Now would have been the time to bring home her son, to settled life in Witham, but Mac's illness and his losing fight with alcoholism made the atmosphere unfavourable.

So, as Dorothy appproached her fortieth birthday, she found a safety-valve for her frustrations and her disappointments in writing. Witham people have spoken of her working away far into the night. **Murder must Advertise** appeared in February, 1933, and Dorothy was already working on **The Nine Tailors.** Her book of short stories, **Hangman's holiday** came out in the same year. No wonder the doctor ordered her to take three weeks holiday, away from writing and away from Mac.

Lord Peter Wimsey, written about for 15 years, was her great benefactor. His creation rewarded her in a very real financial sense, so that she could now write as she pleased and she could afford all the good things in life, especialy in regard to food and drink. Her religious background and her continuing belief encouraged her to accept a commission to write a play in verse, **The Zeal of Thy House**, for performance in Canterbury Cathedral in June, 1937. In 1938 she published in the **Sunday Times, The Greatest Drama Ever Staged in the Official Creed of Christendom.** Its full title explains her message clearly, but it has been known ever since only by its first five words. It was in 1940 that the BBC first mooted the idea of a series of short plays which led to the writing and broadcasting of the famous **The Man Born to be King.** In the same year her comedy **Love All** was put on in a London theatre, but it was smothered by the blitz. Mac, meanwhile, continued ill, moody and, at times, a little unbalanced. Yet he lingered on until he died on 9th June, 1950. In later life Dorothy admitted that her 'irritable and domineering spirit' had sometimes got the better of her. It may have been the reason for her getting involved in religious argument, which brought her more than her fair share of correspondence with bigots, cranks and neurotics.

In 1943 her life changed dramatically, and all through reading a book about Dante, **The Figure of Beatrice**, by Charles Williams and talked about with friends in her house at Witham when they were refugees from the 'doodle-bugs' then falling on the London area. She turned to Dante himself, was quite carried away with what he wrote and how he wrote it and determined there and then to translate into English verse his **Commedia**, supplying a brilliant and informed commentary. It occupied her almost totally from 1945, and she had not quite finished it at her death, when Barbara Reynolds completed it as a labour of love and as an acknowledgment of its considerable contribution to literature. **The Just Vengeance**, commissioned in April, 1945, for the 750th Anniversary of Lichfield Cathedral was much influenced by the total immersion in Dante, though she acknowledged she could not match his simplicity of expression. Her very last play, **The Emperor Constantine**, produced in Colchester in 1951, caused Dorothy endless problems to get it staged and its reception was somewhat affected by its length. It lasted 4 hours or so, with 25 scene changes.

Essex people can take some pride in the fact that it had been conceived in Witham and produced in Colchester, because at this time Dorothy was so absorbed in the Dante translation that she had little time for the outside world. Much of her spare time was devoted to the organisation and continuing administration of St Anne's House in Dean Street, in London, a mission house putting on lectures, talks, meetings; reaching out to agnostics and unbelievers. Up to her death, Dorothy could be said to be the prime mover and the guiding spirit.

Her son, Anthony, was by this time 27 years old and the idea that he would ever come to live as part of the family had long since been relinquished. They were as close as they ever would be on the occasion of Ivy's death, less than a year after Mac. Though Ivy had left everything to Dorothy, she immediately handed it on to Anthony, for Ivy was more mother to him than she could ever be.

Dorothy's own death took place unwitnessed in the house in Witham she had come to love. On 17th December, 1957, she had been to London to do some Christmas shopping, leaving directions for some of the gifts to be delivered. She could have stayed on in Town, but wanted to get back to feed her beloved cats. Jack Lapwood, her favourite driver, met her at Witham Station and drove her home. She had gone upstairs to take off her outdoor clothes and had only reached the foot of the stairs again and the hallway, when she collapsed through a massive stroke and died immediately. For Dorothy, the ever-active, it was a good way to go. Let a quotation from James Brabazon's biography be her epitaph: "Large of body, large of personality, loud of voice and loud of laughter, her death made a large gap in many lives."

Vic Gunn on the water cart about 1922

"Those ancient bells in the steeple
A million times have rung
Their message is clear, I am here, I am here,
Won't you come, won't you come, won't you come."

Vic Gunn.

Let me, in the last section of this book, limn the life of a man who was born and bred, married and buried in Essex; a man whose very anonymity in life and work in the heart of the Essex countryside is a true reflection of the history of countless thousands of Essex people for all the time spanned by the characters described in these pages.

Vic Gunn was a lorry-driver-turned-farmer who wrote poetry. One November evening my wife and I set out to meet his son, Colvin; travelling through fog banks looming in our headlights and parting like curtains veiling the past. At Leaden Roding we turned on to the Dunmow Road, looking for Keeres Green, finding the narrow lane at the second attempt and were welcomed by a voice calling through the darkness at Cut Elms Farm. Colvin had brought a torch to light our way through the yard, for it was as dark out in the country that night as when Vic Gunn himself, as a young man, would virtually have had to feel his way home.

Colvin and his wife made us comfortable before a log fire, brought out bits and pieces from drawers and cupboards to refresh their memory and told us the story of Vic Gunn. Though he lived here for much of his life, Vic was born at Buckhurst Hill on 9th March, 1907, son of James Gunn, gardener to Mr Pelly in one of the big houses that looked out on to Epping Forest. We were shown the book bearing the inscription 'Special Prize awarded to V Gunn by F R Pelly, Esq., for excellence in attendance. Std.2' It was given at Buckhurst Hill Boys' school at the end of Christmas Term, 1915, when he was 8 years old. Shortly after this glow of glory, his father had an altercation with Mrs Pelly, was asked by her husband to apologise, but, being an independent Essex man knowing he was in the right, walked out and made his way to a better future at Margaret Roding. There he rented White Hall Farm, which at least gave him and his growing family a roof over their heads. The war had given agriculture a bit of a boost and James had also taken on extra work as a haulage contractor to help pay his way. By 1919 he was quite well established in the area.

Thus it was that Vic transferred to the village school at Margaret Roding and met his match, literally, in the shape of a pretty little schoolmate who was to become his wife. As the boys grew up, Ralph, Percy, Vic and Albert, and the girls, Nell and Lyn, for that matter, they were set to work on the farm or in the developing transport business which proved James' acumen and foresight. Vic, at 14, said goodbye to school for good and worked on the lorry or the farm as Dad directed. Like his brothers, and his father himself, Vic worked for a mere pittance, and for all the hours deemed needful. It was nothing to him as a lad to be told to help with the haymaking, dawn to dusk over a bank holiday weekend, while his friends were away across the fields on pleasure bent. But when opportunity offered, Vic enjoyed fun and games. The Gunn boys were hard up, but they were well fed and strong as the proverbial ox; the champions for miles around in running and in cycling. Vic was also an accredited ace with the catapult. One day he was employed carting materials for road repair. The gang was resting during dinner break, sprawled either side of the road on the grassy verge. Vic saw a slug slowly moving between the out spread legs of a prostrate, dozing labourer. He let fly with his catapult, squashed the slug - and left the labourer gasping with shock!

On through the 'twenties the farm struggled on and the haulage firm paid its way, with horses supplemented from 1919 by a powerful Foden steam lorry. Then Vic had to learn to drive the Chevrolet his father had bought to replace the Foden. That was in 1927 and, all this time from leaving school, Vic had kept his tryst with Bertha Tyler. When he was not strolling with her through the Margaret Roding countryside, he could be seen, crouched low over his bicycle handlebars, tearing all over the county friendly with and emulating, Vic Simpson, a locally-famous racing cyclist who ran a shop at Leaden Roding. Our Vic was a good-looking, lively man of 26 when he led his bride through the amazing, decorated Norman doorway of Margaret Roding church on 17th June, 1933. They settled down at Brown's Farmhouse at Leaden Roding where Colvin was born. Soon they joined Vic's parents, who had left White Hall for Nether Street Farm in Abbess Roding, also renting Cut Elms farm and White Roding Mill.

Business was doing well enough around 1935 for James to buy the Windmill, an Aythorpe Roding public house that had closed down. In the garden he built a new house he called West View, now known as West Point. He then rented it to Vic who was so settled in the marital mould that Colvin remembers how his father's prized Rudge cycle actually went rusty. Vic enjoyed other homely hobbies when time from work permitted. He was interested in collecting stamps and coins, and he made one or two special friends with whom he could talk about more personal matters, such as his growing interest in poetry. From his father, who died in 1952, Vic inherited strength of mind and kindliness to all men. His sensitivity may have come from his mother. It is hard to imagine a lorry-driver, working all the hours God sends, jotting down in rare moments of leisure, thoughts that had occurred to him whilst on the job, and rendering them in verse.

During World War II, James carried on the business with Vic as his right-hand man, ferrying loads of corn and chalk and beer and what-you-will for factors like Hasler's of Dunmow. At the same time Vic kept up correspondence with men from the area who had been made prisoners-of-war, sending them cigarettes and other comforts when he could. He became well-known in the village for raising money for the welcome-home fund, including fondly-remembered fetes at Aythorpe Roding Rectory with money-spinning sideshows. It was at this time that Vic and his family started going to church more regularly, culminating in Vic's appointment as Church warden, a post to which he was constantly re-elected over a period of 30 years. Vicars came and went; they found that Vic was a man they could rely on for continuity, and for cutting the grass in the churchyard.

Vic had corresponded occasionally with his nephew, Jim Hasler, and they both attempted a little humorous verse in their letters. Another man who influenced him strongly was Jack Shearman of Peppers Green, or Pinches, as it was formerly known. He was an older man with a leaning to learning who may well have given Vic confidence to write his verses down. Some ten years after Colvin's birth, Vic's family was completed with the arrival of a daughter. Happiness indeed, but within two years a certain sadness overtook him, for it was in 1949 that road transport was nationalised and James Gunn & Son was taken over by the state. Victor could not work in these conditions and his father was overdue for retirement, so Vic bought Cut Elms Farm, which they had been leasing, including the farmhouse, two cottages and the stockyard on which Colvin's house was later built, along with 36 acres of good Essex soil. For all his life-long involvement with transport and things mechanical Vic, now 42 years old, turned his hand to farming and made a go of it, growing potatoes, sugar beet, wheat, barley, cabbages and the like.

It was on the tractor that there came to Vic the germ of one of his earliest long poems, dated 1953:

ESSEX PRIDE

"BILL BROWN

There are still a few old fashioned farmers about but, alas, they are fast dying out, for they are the salt of the earth.

I know an old farmer, his name's Bill Brown,
And he farms round Dunmow way,
With main and might works half the night,
As well as all the day.

Now Bill he's got a mixed farm,
With pigs, and hens, and cows,
And he's no fool, but of the old school
Who scorns tractors and combines and six furrow ploughs.

"I can't abide the things" he'd say,
"The rattle and the stink,
And if I bought a milking machine
What would my old cows think?
Can't you see what I mean?
Not milked in the morn by hands that are warm,
But grabbed hold on by a horrible sheen!

"And then there's that old 'lectric,
I wouldn't have it in the place,
And if I bought a motor car
My old mare I'd never face.
A horse you see is faithful,
Just like my old sheep dog,
And a motor car won't get you far
When you are lost in a pea soup fog..."

The poem continues for 7 more verses before ending:

"And that's just a few of the reasons why
Until my dying day,
And as long as I'm the lad of my dear old dad,
I'll do things the old fashion way."

Well, that is the tale of old Bill Brown,
Who will never be understood,
Not in an age when it's all the rage
To use plastic instead of wood.

> But Bill always swears by his old grey hairs
> We shall never be short of grub,
> Not as long as he's got his old granfather's scythe
> And what's left of his sharpening rub."

In 1957 a severe illness slowed Vic up. He had to give up his hobby of archery and his growing interest in crossbows - he had actually made some himself. But he still fulfilled to the letter his duties as Churchwarden and kept the farm in good shape. In 1959 he mused on the lack of understanding between townsman and countryman in **Blessings**:

> "Have you ever heard the townsman talk
> Of the countryman's life of charm?
> How he gets good pay for the few hours a day
> He tiffles around on a farm.
>
> Of course they choose to forget
> That when it's cold, windy and wet
> There is always some job to be done.
> Oh no, these bods from the towns
> Think when you don't ride to hounds
> You just saunter about with a gun.
>
> Well, let each man go his separate way.
> The townsman to office, factory and shop,
> His country cousin to the land,
> To barn, and flock, and crop.
> But let each one to the other
> A friendly hand extend,
> And regard him as a brother,
> For each on each depend."

About 1970, having been desperately ill again, and with his children long grown up and settled in their own lives, Vic sold all his land but one field, the one adjoining Cut Elms Farm, so Colvin and his family can still gaze out upon its greenness in grateful memory. Victor Gunn died in 1978. Six years before that he was able to have published in the slimmest of paperbacks, 11 of his favourite poems. They are not the polished products of a poet laureate, but the feelings of a humble man who liked living in Essex and had a lovely sense of humour. If only we could say back to him his last verse of his

ESSEX PRIDE

Ode to an Unknown Lady:
"Beauty they say is only skin deep.
You have an inner glow,
A personality good and sweet
That makes you so nice to know."

Vic Gunn: lorry driver - farmer - poet

Abbess Roding	159	Keeres Green	**157**
Althorne	124	Langdon Hills	3
Audley End	46	Latchingdon	145
Aythorpe Roding	159,160	Layer Marney	80
Baddow, see Great Baddow		Leaden Roding	157,159
Beauchamp Roding	97	Leigh	32,54
Billericay	4	Little Dunmow	102
Bocking	64	Little Easton	**102**
Bradwell-juxta-Mare	62	Little Woodham, see Woodham Mortimer	
Braintree	33,**64**,81,84,**114**		
Brentwood	3,**10**,**16**	Loughton	54
Buckhurst Hill	158	Maldon	58,62,84,85
Castle Hedingham	77	Margaret Roding	158
Chelmsford	72,**74**,80,85,94,95,101,108,**141**	Markshall	**33**
		Mayland	**123**
Cock Clarks	89,90	Messing	79
Coggeshall	4,33,34	Northey Island	62
Colchester	5,18,**22**,**27**,34,80,155	Pebmarsh	65
Cold Norton	89	Peppers Green	160
Corringham	3	Plaistow	53
Cranham	49	Purleigh	**87**
Cressing	3,109	Puttocks End	127
Earls Colne	33	Rivenhall	**18**
East Ham	53	Saffron Walden	**46**,80
Eastwood	30	Salcot	95
Epping	54	Sewardstone	54
Fairstead	20	Silver End	121,122
Finchingfield	**36**	South Weald	12
Fobbing	3	Stanford-le-Hope	3
Gestingthorpe	77,**133**	Thaxted	30
Gosfield	69	Tilbury	80
Great Baddow	**1**,89	Tiptree	73,92
Great Canfield	127	Tollesbury	93
Great Dunmow	79,82,102	Tollesunt Darcy	**92**
Great Totham	70,92	Upminster	49
Great Waltham	100	Waltham Abbey	4.53,80
Hadleigh	54,80	Walthamstow	**5**
Halstead	37,**64**	White Roding	158
Harlow	113	Widford	**108**
Helmans Cross	127	Witham	70,**82**,**148**
Hempstead	53	Woodford	5
Heybridge	70,73	Woodham Mortimer	**39**,**44**
High Easter	98,101	Writtle	27
Hintlesham	23		

Afford, Bernard Clark	87	Chancellor, Frederic	**74**
Alexander, William	**44**	Chancellor, Wykeham	75
Alexandra, Queen	104	Charles I	32,42
Algar	1	Charles II	42,46
Arch, Joseph	106	Charles V	7
Ascham, Giles	8	Cheek, Mary	83
Ascham, Roger	5	Cheek, Richard Sutton	**82**
Augustine, Saint	62	Clare, John	72
Ball, John	2	Clark, Charles	**70**
Bampton, Thomas	3	Clark, Robert	70
Bardin, Anne	64	Clarkson, Thomas	**141**
Battell, Andrew	32	Cocke, Mary	17
Bastwick, John	**27**	Coke, John	89
Beadell, James	74	Cournos, John	152
Belknap, Sir Robert	3	Courtauld, Augustine	64
Bell, Fanny	130	Courtauld, George	65
Bewley, John	143	Courtauld, Samuel	**64**
Blackie, -	116	Courtauld, Sir William	69
Blatchford, Robert	106	Crittall, Frank	**114**
Bolingbroke, G	76	Crittall, Richard	116
Bonner, Bishop	10	Crittall, Valentine	119
Boswell, James	52	Cromwell, Oliver	58,103
Bright, Edward	**58**	Dalley, Henry	17
Brocket, -	15	Darcy, Sir Robert	62
Brooke, Richard	17	Day, John	86
Browne, Sir Antony	12	De Hispania, Richard	36
Browne, Wistan	16	De Vere, John	80
Brydges, Sir Egerton	73	Denny, Sir Anthony	7
Bryhtnoth	62	Du Cros, Arthur	108
Burgoyne, John	36	Duke, Laura Mary	92
Burke, Edmund	52	Dunn, J S	70
Callis, Charles	18	Durrant, E	76
Capel, Herbert	141	Dyer, Arthur	117
Campbell, Mrs.Patrick	104	Eadwine	1
Caroline, Queen	109	Edward VII	103
Carter, Ellen Laura	117	Elizabeth I	7,22
Carter, Richard	45	Ewell, John	3
Carwardine, Henry	40	Fels, Joseph	124
Cecil, Sir William	8	Fleming, Oswald	152
Cedd, Saint	62	Foster, Raven	37
Chamberlen, Hope	42,44	Foxe, John	35
Chamberlen, Hugh	42	George V	103
Chamberlen, Peter	**39**	Gilberd, Ambrose	22
Chamberlen, William	40	Gilbert, Jerom	22

Gilberd, Thomas	23	Lee, Edward	7
Gilberd, William	**22**	Mary I	10
Giles, Farmer	53	Mason, Jimmy	**127**
Gilroy, John	153	Mason, Richard	127
Goldsmith, Oliver	52	Mason, Tommy	128
Grave, Henry	16	Maude, Aylmer	89
Gregory, -	54	Maynard, Frances	**102**
Greville, Francis	104	Meade, Isaac	**97**
Gunn, Colvin	157	Michell, Emma Carolina	109
Gunn, Vic	**157**	Michell, Frederick	110
Gunther, Phillipa	36	Mellitus, Saint	62
Gwynn, Nell	103	Middleton, Jane	42
Hakluyt, Richard	30	Minton, Jane	65
Hales, Sir Robert	3	Monox, Sir George	5
Hall, -	56	Moon, Amy	19
Harrington, Isaac	118	Mori	
Harris, Sir Arthur	39	Morice, James	16
Harris, Sir Cranmer	39	Morysin, Sir Richard	8
Harrison, Anne	42	Mynto, John	17
Harrison, John	119	Newberry, John	66
Hasler, Jim	160	Newman, John	117
Henry II	39	Nunn, -	89
Henry VIII	2,7	Oates, L E G	**133**
Hone, William	90	Ogier, Louisa	65
Honywood, Hester	34	Oglethorpe, James	**49**
Honywood, Margaret	**33**	Paget, William	19
Honywood, Robert	33	Palmer, Hester	53
Honywood, Sir Thomas	34	Parmenter, -	119
Howard, James	46	Pattisson, J H	82
Howe, Margaret	8	Pelly, F R	158
Hunter, Robert	14	Phillips, William	44
Hunter, William	**10**	Plume, Thomas	62
Jacobs, Samuel	52	Ponde, Richard	15
James I	22,30,42	Poole, Isaac	70
Johnson, George W	70	Purchas, Samuel	**30**
Katharine of Aragon	2	Purchas, Thomas	33
Kemball, Mrs	39	Raglan, Lord	111
Kempe, Robert & Elizabeth	36	Richard II	4
Kempe, William	**36**	Sackville, Sir Richard	8
Kenworthy, John	88	Sales, Mrs	132
King, Tom	53	Salisbury, John	20
Knightbridge, John	75	Salter, John Henry	**92**
Lapwood, John	156	Sayers, Dorothy L	**148**
Le Clerk, John	89	Scott, Robert Falcon	135

Scrope, Lord	6	Tyler, Wat	2
Sewell, John	4	Vassal, Asser	33
Shave, Mrs	115	Vassal, John	32
Shrimpton, Ivy	149	Vaux, Miss	154
Sheldon, -	55	Victoria, Queen	71,103
Sinclair, William	88	Walford, Cornelius	73
Simpson, Vic	159	Walpole, Robert	52
Slack, -	45	Wardrop, Margaret	77
Smith, John Russell	73	Waters, Robert	35
Smith, Robert	84	Western, Thomas	18
Smith, Susan Jane	101	Westwood, Jane	128
Smith, Thomas	123	Wheeler, -	54
Southwell, Pauline	112	Whelpton, Eric	151
Southwell, Sir Robert	19	William I	1
Taylor, Elizabeth	47	Wilson, Sir John Maryon	128
Taylor, Ellen	69	Wingfield, Sir Anthony	6
Taylor, Harold	109	Winstanley, Henry	**46**
Taylor, Peter	66	Winstanley, Thomas	46
Turpin, Dick	**52**	Witts, -	65
Tusser, Edmund	20	Wood, Henry Evelyn	77,**108**
Tusser, Thomas	**18**,73	Wood, John Page & Emma	109
Tyler, Bertha	159	Wren, Sir Christopher	46
Tyler, Thomasine	16	Wright, Elizabeth	51